ENCOUNTERING
THE WILD

ENCOUNTERING THE WILD

CAROL BENNETT McCUAIG

NATURAL HERITAGE BOOKS
A MEMBER OF THE DUNDURN GROUP
www.dundurn.com

Editor: Jane Gibson
Design: Jennifer Scott
Printer: Webcom

Library and Archives Canada Cataloguing in Publication

McCuaig, Carol Bennett
    Encountering the wild / Carol Bennett McCuaig.

Includes bibliographical references and index.
ISBN 978-1-55488-858-0

1. Animals--Anecdotes. 2. Wildlife attracting. 3. McCuaig, Carol Bennett. I. Title.

QL791.M355 2011   590   C2010-907734-2

1 2 3 4 5   15 14 13 12 11

Conseil des Arts du Canada   Canada Council for the Arts

Canadä

ONTARIO ARTS COUNCIL
CONSEIL DES ARTS DE L'ONTARIO

We acknowledge the support of the **Canada Council for the Arts** and the **Ontario Arts Council** for our publishing program. We also acknowledge the financial support of the **Government of Canada** through the **Canada Book Fund** and **Livres Canada Books**, and the **Government of Ontario** through the **Ontario Book Publishers Tax Credit program**, and the **Ontario Media Development Corporation**.

Care has been taken to trace the ownership of copyright material used in this book. The author and the publisher welcome any information enabling them to rectify any references or credits in subsequent editions.

J. Kirk Howard, President

Photography by DW McCuaig and courtesy of the author's collection.

Published by Natural Heritage Books
A Member of The Dundurn Group

Printed and bound in Canada.
www.dundurn.com

Dundurn Press
3 Church Street, Suite 500
Toronto, Ontario, Canada
M5E 1M2

Gazelle Book Services Limited
White Cross Mills
High Town, Lancaster, England
LA1 4XS

Dundurn Press
2250 Military Road
Tonawanda, NY
U.S.A. 14150

MIX
Paper from
responsible sources
FSC® C004071

In memory of another nature lover, my mother,
Hilda Barratt Austin, who died in 2005

CONTENTS

THE SETTING

Renfrew County, located in the Upper Ottawa Valley, is the largest county in Ontario. It is comprised of two million acres of land, more than half of which is under private ownership. Six-hundred-thousand acres of this land are forested, and there are over two hundred lakes and thousands of wetlands within its boundaries.

Ruggedly beautiful, the county is rich in history — particularly with regard to the lumbering days of the nineteenth and early twentieth centuries. Logs were floated down the rivers here: the Ottawa, the mighty Madawaska, and the lovely little Bonnechere. It is said that many a drowned river driver lies in an unmarked grave on the banks of these rivers, having fallen victim to the hazards of this work. These rivers were the first highways in the territory, once the ancestral home of the Algonquin First Nation. The early settlers, mainly French, Irish, and Scots, used these rivers to travel from place to place, long before this became a separate county. Later, immigrants from Poland and Prussia travelled a pioneer trail known as the Opeongo Road, which began at the Ottawa River and ran up through the back country, almost to the limits of what is now Algonquin Provincial Park.

Within living memory it was customary for men from the area to "go to the shanty," which meant that they spent the winter in the lumber camps, leaving their wives and children behind to manage the farms. This enabled their families to supplement their meagre income that came from farming submarginal land. More than fifteen hundred farms are still worked within the boundaries of Renfrew County today. Much of the remaining land, which previous owners found too rocky for productive farming, is ideal for recreational purposes. The area teems with wildlife and birds, and many beautiful, sometimes rare, plants and flowers grow here.

Under the leadership of the Renfrew County Stewardship Council, landowners, organizations, and agencies share a commitment to responsible land care, recognizing that all of us, as well as wildlife and plants, depend on a healthy ecosystem. The Council is part of Ontario Stewardship, an Ontario Ministry of Natural Resources program that encourages the sustainable use of natural resources in the province. Priorities here include the sustainment of forestry, wetlands, wildlife, lakes, and rivers. Stewardship projects, workshops, and conferences provide ways in which interested landowners and school children can participate in the protection of our natural resources and grow in their understanding of the world around us.

Carol Bennett McCuaig lives on a 250-acre property in Admaston Township in Renfrew County. Whimsically known as Poison Ivy Acres, it contains a variety of habitats, including wetlands, ponds, hardwood and softwood bush, rolling hills, and open fields. Many forms of wildlife share this place, where people, pets, animals, and birds have learned to co-exist peacefully — most of the time!

For more than thirty years the author has enjoyed fascinating encounters with numerous animals and birds here. Whether one lives in the country, or only wishes that that were possible, all are invited to share these experiences with her through the pages of this book. The author looks forward to hearing from readers who may have their own encounters with wildlife to share with her.

THE BACKGROUND

Poison Ivy Acres

Poison Ivy Acres is located in the bush country of the Upper Ottawa Valley. It consists of two-and-a-half pioneer farms, first settled by French families who had come from Quebec. The property includes a variety of wetlands, including ponds, swamps, and a creek. In addition to sixty-five acres of open fields, it also has sections of softwood bush and hardwood forest, which means that many different creatures make the area their home.

DW McCuaig, my husband, first purchased the property as a weekend retreat, back in the 1970s. He enjoyed country auctions, and, having heard that a farm couple in the township were having a sale, he turned up to attend it, only to learn that he had come to the wrong place on the wrong day. It proved to be the happiest of mistakes.

When he got out of the car to explain what he was doing on private property so far off the road, he was given a real country welcome by the elderly owners and invited to look around. He loved the place on sight, with its log buildings dating from pioneer days, the creek below the house, and trees as far as the eye could see. No other habitation was visible at all. Best of all was the long avenue of maples, framing the lane on the way in. It was those trees that made him long to have the property for himself.

The acreage was not for sale at the time, but the owners promised to let him know if they ever decided to sell. One day he received the long-awaited phone call, and, in 1971, the property became his. He paid $10,500 for the house and land, which caused great knee-slapping mirth among the farmers of the district. They thought he was a fool to pay so much, and didn't hesitate to tell him so. From their point of view, it might have appeared to be the case. The house had no electricity or water, and only a fraction of the rocky land was under cultivation. However, for someone keenly interested in wildlife and photography, as he was, it was cheap at the price. As for the house, it was a good, solid log building, more than a century old, and ripe for renovation. Believed to have been constructed by those early French pioneers, it had been added to in the 1880s by settlers who had come from Prussia.

Under DW's direction, the house was completely gutted and the logs were stripped down. Seven layers of wallpaper and several coats of paint were removed, including the pioneer milk paint, which is almost impossible to eradicate. Traces of it can still be seen on the logs today. New floors were installed downstairs, made from Nepean sandstone. A large

The house, as it was in 1972. This photo shows the main part of the house, built by French pioneers circa 1860, and the west wing added on by Prussian settlers in the 1880s.

fireplace, constructed from rocks found on the farm, has been much admired by people who come to the house. The Dutch craftsman who built it was so delighted with the result that when he had visitors from Holland he invited them out to see his handiwork.

A smaller log house was brought from five miles away and added on as a new east wing. This, too, had an interesting history. Dating from the time of the Irish potato famine, it had been built by four brothers from County Kerry. After arriving in the township, the brothers lived there together until each one took up an adjoining hundred acres of his own. For some years, that house had been used as a hunt camp, but not maintained year-round. Some of the logs had rotted, but there were almost enough good ones remaining to build the required three walls. However, they needed one more log. The building crew were at a loss about what to do, until the oldest member of the team spoke up.

"I'll show you young whippersnappers how it's done!"

Taking down the big broadaxe that still hangs over the fireplace, he marched outside. Having found a suitable tree, he squared it off before returning to the house with it in

DW and the author out for a hike in the woods. With so much rock in Renfrew County there is always a place to sit down.

triumph. That log is still part of the wall today, complete with the adze marks he had made to match those that the Irishmen had made in the other logs well over a century earlier.

Being interested in the local wildlife, DW began writing a weekly newspaper column that mentioned the small creatures he found on the farm, which included rodents and shrews in particular. He wrote in a chatty style, which appealed to readers. Needing a name for the property, which he frequently mentioned in the column, he came up with the name Poison Ivy Acres, as a joke. The name caught on, and from time to time people still address letters with that name, even though it bears no resemblance to the current civic address.

The column stopped when DW sold his chain of weekly newspapers later in the 1970s. Times were changing, and, to his disappointment and that of many of his readers, the new owners were not interested in wildlife news. In the meantime, I had come on the scene, a countrywoman to the core. We moved, with our assorted dogs, to live full time on Poison Ivy Acres. More refinements were made to the house and grounds as befitted day-to-day occupation, and the old pioneer dwelling took on a new lease of life.

Now the wheel has come full circle, and once more a record is being made of the creatures who visit Poison Ivy Acres.

A Country Child

When I was five years old and growing up in Wales, my young aunt, then aged nineteen, gave me a three-volume set of bird books as a birthday gift, *The Birds of Britain and their Eggs*. I suspect that being short of money, she had purchased these from a second-hand shop, since they were wildly unsuitable for a child just starting school. Nevertheless, I was delighted with these books with their old engravings of stern-looking birds, and I have them still. Neither of us could have had any idea that, years later, I would be writing a weekly newspaper column dealing with the Canadian birds I love so well.

Perhaps recognizing that it would be many years before I could cope with the erudite language and scholarly approach of the books, my parents began buying me a series of nature books designed for children, filled with simple information and brightly coloured illustrations. Before long, I was wandering in the nearby woods and fields, observing birds and animals, and hunting for wildflowers before returning home, where I tried to identify what I had seen with the aid of my books.

One of the highlights of my young life was coming upon a vixen with her cubs in the open country beyond the wood. Lying on my stomach in the long grass, I watched the young foxes at play for what seemed like hours. The scolding I received for coming home late for tea was well worth it. I went back on several occasions, but the foxes never appeared again.

Wandering through the Welsh countryside on horseback, or on foot with the dogs, I saw many things which interested me. Little wonder then that I grew up to become a keen amateur naturalist. Coming to Canada as a young woman meant that I had to begin all over again, because so much of the wildlife is different here, particularly the birds. But far from being a setback this was a delight, because, as any nature-watcher knows, spotting something new is a thrill.

At first I couldn't afford to buy the field guides I craved, but the local library had a copy of Peterson's *A Field Guide to the Birds* and, fortunately, patrons were allowed to take it home on loan. This gave me a wonderful start in my quest to learn more about Canada's rich wildlife.

My mother, too, had an interest in nature, and when I was young she befriended a hedgehog she named Tiggy, in honour of Beatrix Potter's "Mrs. Tiggywinkle." Tiggy was not a pet, in the sense that a pet is usually kept in captivity, as in the case of a rabbit or guinea pig. She (or he, as the case may have been) visited the garden, and came and went at will. Every day at eleven o'clock, Mother made herself a cup of milky coffee and, on fine days, she sat outside to drink it, enjoying the fresh air. How it started I can't recall, but as soon as she sat down, Tiggy would come trundling out of the undergrowth to beg for a saucer of *café au lait*. She also adored gorgonzola cheese!

Tiggy loved to sit on Mother's lap to have her tummy rubbed. Despite the prickles on their backs, hedgehogs are beautifully soft underneath and can be picked up easily if they condescend to allow it. Otherwise they roll into a spiny ball as a means of defence when threatened. Tiggy and Mother carried on many happy conversations of the "tut tut" variety. That is to say, you can imitate a hedgehog by making sucking sounds with the tongue at the back of your upper teeth.

My mother's maternal grandmother, Frances Savin, who died long before my time, also had an affinity for wildlife. She raised an orphaned fox, which followed her everywhere like a little dog and was even allowed inside the house. She also had a pet Jackdaw. Jackdaws, a European corvid, are highly intelligent birds, known to be attracted to bright objects. They can also be taught to speak, and this particular bird was no exception. The younger boys in the family took great delight in teaching the bird to cause trouble. Their father had a workshop at the end of their very long garden, and on several occasions, he rushed down to the house, fearing a domestic emergency, having heard a hoarse voice calling, "Will! Will! Fanny wants you!" When his wife expressed surprise at seeing him, they concluded that it was "that dratted bird again."

My own grandmother, who was a child when Fanny befriended these wild creatures, used to regale me with tales of their appearance within the family circle. With such a heritage, is it any wonder that I have an interest in nature?

A Carefree Naturalist

I wear the mantle of amateur naturalist quite lightly. To begin with, although I like to think of myself as fairly knowledgeable about the species I observe on a daily basis, I am not a biologist or a professional ornithologist. High-school biology classes did not contribute a great deal to my fund of knowledge; better by far were the elementary-school lessons based on the items that were contributed to the nature table by eager pupils. I suppose that, even then, I preferred hands-on experiences to textbook materials.

In my time, I have belonged to field naturalist groups and participated in their outdoor activities. I have watched wildlife documentaries on television and enjoyed countless books and magazine articles. For more than forty years, I have joined in the local Christmas Audubon Bird Counts. I have even been on birding expeditions in Texas and in Ireland. All these have provided food for the soul.

However, I am not the sort of person who spends cramped hours in a duck blind, or crouching behind a tree hoping to spot a certain bird or animal. Nowadays, I let them come to me, and very often they do so. Beside the window of my home office, there is an Amur Maple on which birds love to perch since my bird feeders are close by. So, I can be typing away happily and then, when I look up, I see some rare bird just a foot or two from my nose. I then can make a note of its field marks without moving from my chair.

Occasionally, if I happen to see a rare or uncommon bird here, I share the news with the man who writes the bird column in our local newspaper. This prompts some readers to exclaim that I must be a really dedicated birdwatcher, but this is hardly the case at all. It's all a matter of luck.

It's the same with wild animals. Quite a few of them come to the house, especially when there is little food for them in the wild. This may be during a season of drought, when berries are scarce, or when there is deep snow with a hard crust. Conditions that

make difficulties for wild creatures often bring me some of my best sightings, and I'm grateful for them.

Having said all that, I should point out that these home-based observations are only part of the picture. Many of my experiences have taken place away from the house, in the woods or out in the fields, and they seldom happen to order. This is not a safari park where visitors can hope to see wolves or mink on demand. My observations have been made over a thirty-year period and, naturally, there are days and even weeks when nothing unusual comes into view.

At the same time, it helps to know where creatures are likely to be at certain times. As the saying goes, "If you want to see a bear, go where a bear is." Winter is the best time to

The author with the gang: Jordie, Bunny, Blue, and Rusty. All the setters were keen swimmers.

see what animals and birds have passed by, since their tracks in the snow tell the story. I'm delighted to share my earthly paradise with them all, and my reward is that every day holds something of interest, as I go out walking or snowshoeing at varying times of the day.

In some ways I'm glad that I don't have any specialized training in nature study. A biologist, looking at animals in the wild, can interpret their behaviour based on what he has been taught. Because I'm not a scientist, anything I can learn through my own observation comes as a delightful surprise.

PART I:
ENCOUNTERS WITH ANIMALS

COURTSHIP OF THE RED FOX

I enjoy meeting animals in the wild. I encounter them every day in the bush. A wolf may stop and stare at me for an instant before moving on; a fawn may peer curiously over a juniper bush; and sometimes, a bear reveals his presence only when I hear him lumbering away through the undergrowth.

I like to watch these creatures, but so far nothing has equalled the experience of the courtship ritual of a pair of Red Foxes (*Vulpes vulpes*) that took place on two successive days, right outside my bedroom window. This was a special privilege because the fox is a reclusive animal. Also, the ritual is completed within thirty-six hours or less, so the chances of it being witnessed by the casual observer are slim indeed.

The winter of 1993–94 was unusually severe. Towards the end of January, the weather turned mild for a few hours, during which a heavy rain fell. By nightfall, the temperature had again dropped below zero, causing the water to freeze. Branches snapped off under the unaccustomed weight of ice; the snow, more than two feet deep, was covered with an iron-hard crust that stayed for some weeks.

One night, I looked out of the bedroom window and saw a fox. It was standing on the flat-topped boulder that we used as a bird feeder. It probably was hoping to catch the small rodents that come out at night to feed on fallen seed. The crust on the snow, which was strong enough to support our seventy-five pound dogs, kept the small mammals trapped underneath and the fox was not strong enough to break through. The fox was reduced to eating bird seed.

In our area, we have learned to be wary of foxes when they come too close to buildings. Normally the fox is a secretive animal, but rabies can be a problem, so it pays to be cautious. This fox, however, looked alert and healthy, although painfully thin. It returned the next night, and the night after that. I didn't want to make the animal dependent on me, yet I didn't want it to starve on my doorstep, either. Deciding that unusual conditions call for unusual measures, I put out a small pile of dry dog food. The fox ate it all.

Encouraged, the fox began coming to the house by day. I put the food on the ground about ten feet from the front of the house, so I could watch the animal from an upstairs window. Its routine never varied: it would take a morsel of food to the shelter of a nearby spruce tree and chew carefully while turning its head in all directions, alert to possible danger. Then it would return for another piece. Fortunately, the fox arrived at the same time

Can you spot the fox?
They are curious crea-
tures that often watch
the author as she goes
about her daily round.

each morning, enabling me to juggle dog walks and fox feeding. Sometimes one of the dogs got wind of the animal outside and barked a warning, and the fox would leave in a hurry.

One morning, I stepped outside, carrying the food in a plastic sandwich bag. The ice had become too treacherous to walk on, so I attempted to throw the food across to the usual spot, while hanging on to the bag. Unfortunately, the wind took it and I was forced to go back indoors, leaving the full bag far out of my reach. When the fox came along he sniffed at the bag, picked it up in his mouth, and trotted away with it. Packed lunches for foxes!

On the eighth of February, while sitting at the computer in my upstairs office at the side of the house, I glanced up and saw what I took to be my fox, sitting bolt upright in a snowbank. This was not its usual behaviour, so I rushed to the front of the house, meaning to throw out some food before it rounded the corner and became startled by the sound of the window opening.

The fox was there before me. Puzzled, I waited at the window and then, out of the corner of my eye, I saw another, smaller fox appear. I soon realized that the fox on the snowdrift must have been a vixen. She sat down about ten feet away from her mate.

Strangely, she did not take any food. She waited patiently until he had eaten his meal, piece-by-piece, and then the courtship ritual began. First, the dog fox established territory by running in a circle, stopping to lift his leg on nearby spruce trees, a stone fence, a dead mullein plant. Then he began sidling up to the vixen and backing off again, shaking his head and dancing. While this was happening she sat watching, with what can only be described as a laugh on her little face. Mouth open, head thrown back, eyes shining.

As he became bolder, the vixen bounded away, stopping after a few yards to look back over her shoulder. Then, as he approached, she tossed her head, pretending not to notice. After half an hour of this display they ran off together, noses to the ground, pursuing that erratic course common to foxes.

The next morning they were back, and the process was repeated. This surprised me because, since they had trotted off together, I had assumed that they were now a confirmed pair. They did not come a third time, although the dog fox returned at night as long as the cold spell lasted. I had hoped to see the young cubs in due course, but perhaps that was asking too much. Red Foxes have only one nursery den, but each family usually maintains numerous lairs as a retreat from predators.

Several winters ago I was lucky enough to find an inhabited den, steam rising from its entrance. One set of fox tracks led to this opening: possibly a pregnant vixen was inside. The female remains in her den while her mate hunts for food.

Foxes are curious creatures. They like to watch me as much as I like to see them. Quite often, I see fox tracks beside my footprints in the snow, indicating that they have followed my scent. Perhaps these prints belong to the descendants of my winter visitors.

THE BEAR FACTS

I had just come in from a walk through the cedar swamp, during which I observed something interesting: rocks had been pulled from the ground and turned over. This meant that a bear has recently passed by, looking under the stones in search of ants — a special treat for bears.

The creatures are not the fearsome Grizzly Bears found in the Rocky Mountains of Western Canada, but a much smaller species, the Black Bear (*Ursus americanus*). Even an outsize male seldom weighs more than four or five hundred pounds, but since that is the combined weight of several humans, it is unwise to confront them in the wild.

There is a saying in our district, "Leave a bear alone and he'll leave you alone," and that is good advice. Much as we all loved our cuddly teddy bears when we were young, a bear in his own habitat is something to be avoided. I enjoy seeing them from the safety of the car when driving down the nearby country roads, but I'd rather not come face to face with one in the bush, especially in the spring when Mama Bear takes her babies for a walk! Bear cubs are born in the winter, weighing less than one pound, but they are considerably larger by the time they are allowed out of the den.

Our dog, Jordie, an English Setter, seemed to sense my diffidence — or perhaps he could scent a bear from some distance away. They have a rancid smell. Anyway, he developed a scream of fury, put to use whenever he got a whiff of bear. To fully appreciate this phenomenon, you need to know that Jordie was an extremely timid dog, which made it all the more strange that he should choose to see off an invader so much bigger than himself.

Once, my younger daughter came home from college for a visit, bringing three other girls with her. They arrived before I had returned from shopping and duly let themselves into the house. Having heard an unfamiliar car approaching, three of the dogs went into their house-guarding routine, but they soon calmed down when Joanna introduced her friends. Not Jordie. He was so alarmed that all he could think of to do was dash round the room, lifting his leg at intervals to mark his territory!

He was as brave as a lion when it came to bears, however. On one occasion, he started screaming when we were walking up a trail through the bush. The next thing I knew, there was a crashing sound as Bruin lumbered away. I hadn't even known that a bear was watching us.

Another time, I was canoeing down the creek, keeping my eyes open for kingfishers and Green Herons, with the dogs trotting along the bank beside me. Jordie suddenly gave voice, and I caught a glimpse of a bear on the opposite bank, running for its life. Given the fact that a bear can out-run, out-swim, and out-climb a human, I can't say that I minded this sudden retreat.

Then there was the autumn in which I had to feed a bear. Any naturalist or campground warden will tell you that this is completely the wrong thing to do. Leaving food around in the open will only encourage bears to come closer to human habitation, making them dependent on handouts instead of foraging for themselves. It also makes them more inclined to approach people, possibly with tragic consequences.

However, this was a special case. There had been a drought all summer, and there were no berries, insects, or other food for wildlife. The wild apple trees a couple hundred yards from the house had already been stripped bare by the deer.

Desperate for something to eat, a large bear began to search for acorns. One night, Jordie sounded the alarm, and I went outside to hear a bear clawing its way up a sixty-foot Bur Oak not far from the house. I tried the well-known tactic of clattering saucepans together to scare the beast off; I even honked the car horn for several minutes, all to no avail. How long would it be before it ventured closer to the house?

In the morning, I inspected the tree and found great gouges in the trunk. A number of upper branches were strewn on the ground. There are more Bur Oaks very close to the house, and I could foresee having Bruin on my doorstep for days to come.

A neighbour gave me pails of windfalls from her orchard; she didn't want bears around her house, either. I spread them on the ground under the bear's favourite wild apple tree, which is at least a quarter of a mile away, and this did the trick. The bear did not return. Needless to say, my friends all thought they were dealing with a madwoman!

However, not long afterwards I heard on the television news that there was trouble on the outskirts of Ottawa, some seventy-five miles from Poison Ivy Acres. City people were complaining that bears were turning up in their gardens, ruining their crops, and raiding their garbage cans.

Something had to be done, and personnel from the Ministry of Natural Resources were called in to deal with the problem. A number of bears were captured, taken away, and released into the wild. And then, because they couldn't be allowed to starve, a program of feeding these animals was started up, to tide them over until denning-up time. So you see, what I did wasn't so foolish after all.

Bears remain in their dens all winter. They don't really hibernate; they just go into a deep sleep. Occasionally, one wakes up during the January thaw and goes outside to stretch its legs. If the creek is open, it will stop to quench its thirst. That's when I sometimes see giant paw prints in the snow, probably made by a male as this is the time when females are occupied, giving birth to their young.

On one occasion, I was making prints of my own, wearing bear-paw snowshoes, but I retreated in a hurry when I came across a pile of bear droppings, still steaming. There are times when discretion is the better part of valour!

BLUE AND THE WOLF

Poor Blue! He didn't appreciate his encounter with a wolf that autumn morning! DW, who had been left alone in the kitchen while I was out walking the dogs, was not expecting us back for some time. Thus, he was amazed to hear a frantic scrabbling at the back door. Seconds later he was even more puzzled to see this normally placid English Setter leaping up at the kitchen window, his claws hitting the glass. When he finally opened the door, the dog pushed past him and collapsed on the floor, wild-eyed and gasping. Something seemed to be badly wrong and it took DW some time to comfort the shuddering animal.

When I reached home, I had to explain what had happened. We have several miles of hiking trails around the property. I had just emerged from the trees where the path I had taken joins the main trail leading to the house when, out of the corner of my eye, I saw Blue racing towards me. He'd been lagging behind and I assumed that he was trying to catch up with the rest of the party.

Thinking he hadn't noticed me, I gave a blast on my whistle, expecting him to come to my side as he always did. But he kept going. It was then that I saw the wolf: a fine grey-coloured specimen a little taller than seventy-five-pound Blue. In the heat of the moment, I couldn't decide whether I was seeing a large Brush Wolf (Coyote) or a Timber Wolf. (I later decided that it must have been the former.) They are known to hybridize with domestic dogs and seldom show any fear of them.

This animal was cantering along with its tongue lolling out, and I sensed that it just wanted to play with the dog, rather than displaying any hostility. Poor Blue obviously thought otherwise. Discretion being the better part of valour, he headed for the safety of home.

Suddenly, the wolf caught sight of me and came to a halt, registering shock. In one swift movement it reversed direction and bounded back down the trail. This was too much for the senior setter, twelve-year-old Bunny. Although crippled with arthritis, he uttered an indignant yelp and gave chase, temporarily rejuvenated by the excitement. He gave up after a quarter of a mile and trotted back, eyes gleaming and honour satisfied. Blue, on the other hand, was jumpy for days.

Delighted by this encounter, and hoping to make a positive identification of the animals I had seen, I studied the books in our home library, without reaching a satisfactory conclusion. Brush Wolves, I learned, run with their tails down, while Timber Wolves carry their tails horizontally. That was no help, because in its headlong flight, my animal's tail was

all over the place. It wasn't until I had a close look at Timber Wolves at a later date that I thought it was probably a Brush Wolf that had chased Blue.

When city people hear this story they are usually alarmed, fearing for my safety. As my experience proves, the wolf was more frightened of me! Local history books are full of stories about pioneers being chased by wolves, often being forced to take refuge up a tree. These tales probably all involved Timber Wolves, who were far more plentiful in those days. Or perhaps, in some cases, the terrified settlers mistook the intentions of these animals, who are still getting bad press after all these years. (Let's not forget what happened to Little Red Riding Hood's grandma!)

A Coyote, known locally as a Brush Wolf, surveys its territory. While they usually congregate in packs, a single animal often ventures near the house.

Probably those wolves did behave in a territorial manner because they were not used to seeing people. Nowadays, their habitat has shrunk and they have learned to fear us, so the roles have been reversed.

In our district, we have two breeds of wolf: the Grey or Timber Wolf (*Canis lupus*) and the Coyote (*Canis latrans*). Both have been seen at Poison Ivy Acres because their territories intersect in this area. While the term Coyote is the official designation for the latter animal, here in the country they are known to residents as Brush Wolves, and that is the name I prefer to use.

At certain times of year, I like to stand outside at night and listen when the howling of the Coyotes and the yapping of their young can sometimes be heard. Anyone who can imitate the Coyote's call is likely to hear a howl in response. One can even "communicate" at length, which is fun to do. Fortunately, we have no neighbours close by to complain about the noise!

There is a creek just below the house and many creatures come there at night to drink. On one occasion, there was a confrontation with the Coyotes howling on one side of the water and the dogs barking back at them from the other. This was no joke because there is an echo down in the valley and the noise seemed to be coming from all sides. This went on for a long time, until my husband, driven to distraction, went to the window and shouted, "Shut up!" to the dogs. Instant silence from the canines of both species. We had to laugh.

I have sometimes come face to face with a solitary Brush Wolf in the bush, and we have simply stopped and looked at each other for a long moment, before continuing on. They have never threatened me in any way, and I consider myself privileged to get a look at these splendid animals once in a while.

A FAWN ARRIVES

Of all the creatures that are born on my land, I think that the fawns are the prettiest, with their red-brown coats and white spots. They are the offspring of the White-tailed Deer (*Odocoileus virginianus*). "White-tailed" refers to the underside of the tail, which flicks up like a flag when the deer bounds off, and probably acts as a signal to others in the group.

I often see several deer on my lawn in the early morning or late evening, and I meet them on the trails at other times of day. They are rather shy creatures whose ears move constantly as they stay alert to danger, yet they will venture close to the house when they suspect that a tulip or some tasty runner beans may be available for a nibble. They also enjoy munching on lilac leaves and Crown Vetch, a ground cover similar to alfalfa. I don't mind sharing the latter with them, because it spreads like wildfire and can be too much of a good thing.

Every spring, I see at least one pair of twins following behind their mother. Typically, does produce just one fawn. When the youngsters are very new, the mother leaves them in a safe place while she goes off to graze; it is only when they are old enough to canter along behind the older deer that they come out of the undergrowth to take a look at the wider world. Despite this safeguarding of the young, I had the most marvellous experience of seeing a newborn fawn close up.

This is how it happened.

I was out for a walk one spring evening, when I heard strange noises coming from behind a thick growth of juniper bushes. Huffing and puffing and grunting. What on earth was it? Could it be a doe, giving birth? Not wanting to intrude, I hurried by, bringing the dogs home by a different path.

The next morning, we retraced our route. When we emerged into open pasture land the first thing I saw was a doe, quietly grazing. I expected her to bound away with a flick of her tail, but the wind was in our favour and she didn't notice me. I moved to the other side of some trees and there, lying on the ground, was a tiny fawn, not much bigger than one of my cats. Its legs were drawn up beneath it and its head was lying on one side. I wondered if it was injured, so I went up to it, being careful not to get too close in case my scent somehow lingered on its coat, causing the mother to reject it.

One anxious brown eye stared up at me, and I understood then that the little creature was trying to defend itself in the only way it knew how, by playing dead or trying to meld into the scenery. I tiptoed away, trusting its parent to look after it.

Half an hour later, leaving the dogs at home, I returned to the spot, just to check that all was well. There was no sign of the doe or the fawn, so I assumed that mother and baby had been reunited.

A couple of years later, I was walking up in the hayfields at quite a distance from the house, when I came upon a grazing doe. Startled, she bounded away. Instead of disappearing into the distance, she stopped, looking back at me, waiting. I moved a step or two, and she repeated the process. *Aha!* I thought. *She has a fawn nearby and is trying to draw me off.* Sure enough, there was a small one lying in a patch of flattened grass. It was alert, and I guessed that it had been born on the spot shortly before.

White-tailed Deer coming down to the creek to drink in early spring when there is open water.

Later that day, I was hiking up the lane, quite far from the fields, when a doe burst out of the woods and crossed in front of me. Wobbling along behind was her spotted baby. It stumbled when its feet met the gravel, but it recovered quickly and carried on. Not for the first time, I considered how remarkable it is that some animals, such as horses and deer, learn to walk when only a few hours old. Just compare this with a human baby who takes its first steps around the age of a year or later!

A rather different encounter took place one summer evening when I went out to the woodshed to fetch a watering can. A large fawn, grazing quietly nearby, failed to notice me.

Its vigilant mother, however, saw me coming. I expected her to bound away with her youngster in tow, which is the usual response to my sudden appearance. In this case, she stood facing me with her back to the fawn, and she remained in that position while I retrieved the watering can and walked back to the house. I am sure that had I come any closer, I would have received a nasty kick.

DW had photographed elephants in Kenya, and these pictures often show a cow elephant standing on the edge of the herd with her back to the rest of the beasts. No doubt these cows were standing on guard, ready to sound the alarm in case of approaching danger. The doe I came across on that summer evening appeared to have the same thing in mind.

I have a keen sense of smell, and when I'm out walking I can often scent where deer have rested shortly before. Some people scoff at this notion, remarking that they can't smell a thing. This, in turn, surprises me. Horses and cattle have a pleasant and distinctive odour, so it stands to reason that other large animals do, too. Perhaps one needs to live in the country to become aware of all its scents, which the urban dweller is unable to identify.

A BEAR ON THE ROOF

Many of my encounters with wildlife begin when I am sitting at my computer. At my right, facing west, there is a window, nine-feet wide, which overlooks the bird feeders. On the south side, there is a dormer window, overlooking the lawn, with a view of the pond beyond. I keep a pair of binoculars on my desk so that when something interesting comes into view, I can get a better look.

However, on the day the bear climbed onto the roof I was totally immersed in my work, tackling a tricky bit of cutting and pasting, and it wasn't until I heard the crash that I realized I was missing something.

A bear, which probably weighed about three hundred pounds, had scaled the big spruce tree outside the open bedroom window, somehow without my noticing what was going on. A branch had given way under its weight and down it came, landing on the ground with an almighty thump. I leapt up and rushed into the bedroom for a closer look and there it was, lying on the grass below, apparently stunned. After a long moment, it shook its head as if in disbelief and hobbled away.

The cats have a big playroom, with screens from floor to ceiling. When this happened, they were lying out there, snoozing in the sun. When the bear crashed to earth just a few feet away from them, they were understandably shocked. There is nothing like having your slumber disturbed by the arrival of a large bear crashing into your dreams. They were on edge for the rest of the day.

I concluded that the bear, unable to find food, had decided to break into the house, and the open window had proved to be too much of a temptation. Bears have been known to eat small mammals, but fortunately it did not have its eye on the cats, for it could easily have broken through the screens into their room, and from there into the main house.

I was thankful that the little episode ended as it did, as bears can create havoc when they get into a building. DW had a fishing camp where a bear had once broken into the cabin there, leaving a trail of destruction. It had smashed a window, so there was broken glass everywhere, and it had clawed its way into a padlocked food cupboard where there was a pail of honey. Could the animal have known that there was honey in that cabin, or did it simply make its way in on the off chance of finding food? One thing is certain: if my unwelcome visitor had succeeded in gaining entry to my home, chaos certainly would have resulted.

My strangest experience with a bear had a flavour of the supernatural about it. A quarter of a mile from the house there is a small pet cemetery where nine of our previous dogs are buried. Having lived to a ripe old age, they are buried there in the surroundings they rejoiced in during their time with us.

When Bunny, my Irish Setter, died, I was unable to dig far enough down in the rocky ground, so his grave was completed with a mound of earth and rocks. Some years later, I had a very vivid dream, in which this dog came to the house. It was lovely to "see" him again, especially as he appeared to be young and lively, with no trace of the arthritis that plagued his final years. We spent a pleasant time together, but at the end of the dream he managed to convey the message that his grave was being desecrated. Then I woke up with a jolt.

The dog had been so insistent that I pulled on some clothes and jogged down to the cemetery, feeling very silly indeed, yet compelled to visit his grave even before my first cup of coffee. When I got there I found that several of the larger stones had been scooped out and scattered about. None of the other graves had been disturbed at all.

It was obvious that the culprit had been a bear, hunting for ants, but that didn't explain my dream. As Hamlet says, "There are more things in heaven and earth, Horatio, than are dreamt of in your philosophy."

A PAIR OF TIMBER WOLVES

I was sitting in the utility room beside the back door, strapping cleats onto my boots. I was about to set out on my daily trek to the mailbox. As I'd discovered the previous day, it was icy underfoot, and I had no wish to fall. I glanced up, my mind on other things, when I noticed two magnificent Timber Wolves (*Canis lupus*) wandering about between the wood-shed and the small log cabin that, in pioneer times, had served as a granary.

I remembered the day when Blue had been chased by a Brush Wolf, a fairly big animal, taller than Blue. In the heat of the moment I had had a difficult time trying to decide if that's what it was, or if indeed it was a Timber Wolf. Having seen this pair, I realized that there is really no comparison between the two species. The Grey Wolf, as it is also known, isn't much bigger than the Brush Wolf, or Coyote, which is a different species of mammal, yet there is something about its attitude and bearing that proclaims its superiority.

Timber Wolves are pack animals, yet for years a lone wolf has been seen in this district and I have seen its tracks in the snow on my lane on countless occasions. By their affectionate behaviour together, I wondered if this was a mating pair, and I was thrilled to see them. At the same time, I was nervous about going outside. But, being too lazy to remove my boots and all my heavy winter clothing only to begin again later, I decided to chance it. The wolves moved off in the direction of the creek, and I shouldered my backpack and headed for the lane.

While they usually don't attack humans, that was a strange winter, when here and there a wolf approached human habitations in search of food. A few miles away from Poison Ivy Acres, a wolf had killed a small dog while its owner watched in horror. The poor beast was tied to its doghouse and had no chance of escaping.

In our own area, parents were, quite naturally, afraid to let their children play outside in places where a different wolf had been spotted. As a result, the Ministry of Natural Resources had given permission for this wolf to be trapped. Unfortunately, Poison Ivy Acres backs onto Crown land, where a local man maintains a trapline, and I feared for the fate of the handsome pair I had seen.

As usual, I followed a set of wolf tracks up the lane and halfway along I found them joined by a second set, leading out of the bush. This, then, was the spot where the two animals had joined forces, although, of course, there was no way of knowing if they were already acquainted before then.

On the way home, I heard the most blood-curdling howls coming from the valley below. These howls were more full-bodied than the sounds I habitually hear from the Brush Wolves. I shuddered, wondering what it meant. Had one of the animals already fallen into a trap, and was now being mourned by its mate? Or was this simply part of the mating ritual? I hurried home, with the melancholy sound ringing in my ears.

A year later, I haven't spotted the pair again, but almost every day there is a fresh set of tracks going up the lane. The question is, am I watching to see what the wolf has been up to, or is he observing me? Perhaps the feeling is mutual!

At the time of writing, January 2010, our local newspaper, *The Eganville Leader*, has just published a lengthy account of a wolf attack in another part of the county, not so many miles from here. A middle-aged couple, experienced outdoors people, were ice fishing when they were approached by a very large wolf, which came in for the attack. They had brought their puppy with them, and it is possible that the wolf had scented it as a possible source of food.

There was no mistaking the fact that the wolf was on the attack. It constantly lunged at the husband, with its enormous teeth snapping. Armed only with an ice chisel, the man managed to hold the animal at bay, while his wife watched in horror, clutching their small dog. Fortunately, after about fifteen minutes, the wolf gave up and left the scene, leaving the shaken pair to hurry back to their truck. What was even more terrifying was that a pack of wolves could be heard howling in the nearby woods. Had more of them joined in the fray, this story could have had a very different ending.

As a forester who has logged in Algonquin Park, the hero of this tale has seen many wolves in his time and nothing like this has ever happened to him before. "A wolf would never approach a human, that's just not normal," he told the newspaper reporter. Furthermore, the brave pair declared that they had no intention of giving up ice fishing because of their bad experience.

A spokesman for the Ministry of Natural Resources later agreed that such contact with a Timber Wolf is extremely rare. He noted that, although people should be vigilant and always prepared while enjoying the great outdoors, they should not fear being approached and should regard this as a very isolated incident.

Amen to that! As for yours truly, perhaps it was just as well that I viewed my pair of wolves from the safety of the house!

A DOG NAMED RUSTY

Once in a lifetime, a special dog comes along, guaranteed to work its way into the heart of any dog lover. Rusty was such an animal.

He came into our lives quite by chance. In our part of the world "the dog-tax man" (or woman, as the case may be) arrives at one's door in the spring, collecting the money for dog licences. Our local man had just handed over the collar tags when he hesitated and said, "I see that you have an Irish Setter and two English Setters. How would you like to complete the group with a Gordon Setter?"

We were intrigued. This Scottish variety is quite handsome, a mixture of red and black. I've heard that these dogs were originally bred by the Duke of Gordon, who crossed Irish Setters with Border Collies.

The tax collector, Richard, told us a sad story. He had just come from a farm where he had seen a beautiful year-old dog who was about to be put down. An elderly couple had received Rusty, then six months old, as a Christmas gift from their son. But now the dog had grown too large for them, and, being untrained, was over-exuberant and tended to flatten the small grandchildren when they came to visit.

This dog lived under the porch, and, with nobody to exercise him, took himself for walks along a busy highway that fronted the farm. Not only was this a danger to himself, but there was always the possibility of a car accident. His owners refused to purchase a tag because, they said, they were waiting for a neighbour, who was a police officer, to come and shoot the dog. Richard begged for a week's stay of execution, hoping that he could find a new home for the animal.

We went to see Rusty, who greeted us like long-lost friends and promptly jumped into the car. He came home with us without a backward glance, which was sad for the lady of the house, who apparently was fond of him. Fortunately, he took to the cats at once. I will draw a veil over what happened when the other dogs met him at the door. He had never been allowed inside his previous home, but all our animals are indoor residents, so he had to be taken in.

DW was tired and he decided to go to bed early. He had no sooner settled down when a black head appeared on the pillow next to him. Rusty was here to stay!

We knew nothing of his previous history. Where had he spent the first six months of his life? Was there a previous owner somewhere, mourning the loss of his pet? We contacted the Kennel Club to see if he could be traced, without success. We think that he must have lived near a fire station, for he became agitated whenever a fire reel passed us, sirens blaring. Police cars didn't have the same effect.

He loved to go out in the car and he behaved beautifully in a canoe. Luckily for him, he was able to indulge both passions in his new life. He was also a very strong swimmer and would plunge into the lake in even the coldest weather.

All this country living meant that the dogs frequently came into the house soaking wet and muddy. The rule was: no lying on the furniture until dry. Soon after he arrived, however, Rusty jumped on the bed in an awful condition and stretched out. The bedding was soaked and had to be washed and dried. Shaking the duvet, I read the riot act. "Look at this, all dirty! *Grr!* You are not to get on this again, do you hear me?"

Whenever he was trying to understand something new, he would put his head on one side and frown. One could almost see the wheels going round in his brain. Did my lecture work? You be the judge!

The next time he leapt up on the bed, he carefully removed the duvet before lying down. I watched him from behind the door: he took the duvet in his teeth and gently pulled it to the bottom of the bed before hopping up to stretch out. When I went in he looked at me with a cheeky grin. "I did what you told me, Missus!" I didn't have the heart to scold him. He had done his best.

When strangers drove into the yard, Rusty was there to warn us. The house has the sort of two-level windows that open by pushing them up or down. Rusty used to take the lock in his teeth to open it, and then push the lower window up. They are fitted with screens so he couldn't fall out, but he could certainly make his presence felt.

Rusty only had to see something once to be able to copy it. He could unlock a door with his teeth and turn a doorknob with his paw. He was fascinated by the inner workings of the car. Of course, if I had to leave him alone in it for a few minutes, I would have to turn the ignition off and take away the key. He usually found something to interest him. I remember one particular time when I came back and started the car, and immediately the left turn signal came on, the windshield wipers started to work, and the tape player burst into song.

By now, the skeptics will be saying that this was all coincidence; he must have flopped against the dashboard or something. Not on your life. He used to watch me doing things and then try to copy me. Like the time he saw me reading a book, when he went to fetch one for himself. He began turning the pages over with his nose, staring inside to see what was so fascinating.

When I took the car to the dealership to be serviced, seventy-five miles from home, Rusty usually came, too. Although I don't eat a lot of meat, and a fast-food meal is a rare thing for me, we often treated ourselves to a cheeseburger apiece before we left the city for the trip back. On one such trip, I requested one with relish and one left plain.

"Are you sure you wouldn't like onions or red peppers?" the helpful teenaged server asked. "Not even ketchup? Why not try a pickle? They're really good!"

"No, thank you. My dog doesn't like pickles."

The boy's gaze went to the window. Rusty could be seen standing in the passenger seat of my car, on the alert for the coming of his treat. "This is for a dog?" He shook his head in disbelief. As I left I could hear him muttering to himself. "A whole cheeseburger! For a dog!"

Rusty, of course, knew nothing of this. He waited quietly as I broke his meat patty into pieces, and then he wolfed it down. He completed his meal by investigating the paper bag, but there was nothing there but an enticing odour.

Our treat was over for another six months, but he seemed to remember that good things came in small paper bags. When I went to the hardware store to buy nails, he was delighted to see a brown paper bag on the floor of the car. When he nosed his way into it and found nothing of interest, the look of disgust he gave me should have been captured on camera. There is nothing like a setter for making a person feel guilty!

Rusty learned to turn off light switches in the house. If the telephone rang too long, he would simply take it off the hook. He had learned that trick from our cat, Blackie Ryan. What a pair! What a dog!

CREATURES GREAT AND SMALL

Years ago, I witnessed a little drama that had the participants baffled. A small boy had poked his head through some iron railings and was unable to back out again because his ears were in the way. A large policeman and other emergency workers were standing around, scratching their heads, while the unfortunate child, held firmly in place, continued to bawl. The onlookers were being moved on, and I trailed after them, so I have no idea how the problem was solved in the end.

As any parent knows, children have a habit of getting themselves into trouble and, in this regard, other mammals are better equipped to extricate themselves from such situations. Of course, one doesn't find animals pushing beads up their noses or swallowing buttons!

I have observed that, unlike the foolish child, many mammals are capable of making themselves small when they want to pass through a space that, to the human eye, looks far too narrow for them. Country dwellers know that this is true of mice and bats, for example. Bats can enter through a space no larger than a quarter of an inch, incredible though this sounds. Mice manage to squeeze through spaces that seem smaller than their heads, alongside water pipes and electrical cables. I'd often wondered how they manage it, until Rusty showed me how.

Our beautiful Gordon Setter was a real escape artist. He did not come to us until he was about a year old, and we soon learned that he suffered from separation anxiety. This was seldom a problem because we both worked in a home office, and when we did have to go to town to shop, he came along. However, a winter day came when he had to be left behind for a few hours, and, because he was still at the stage where he quarrelled with the other dogs, he was left in our comfortable guest house, where the windows are low enough for him to look out. Here, we thought, he could be warm and comfortable until our return. We came home to find all the curtains pulled down from the windows and the hooks sprung into unrecognizable shapes.

The next time we left him, we put him outside in the seldom-used dog pen. It is a small log building, formerly a calf pen, surrounded by chain-link fencing, seven-feet high. Satisfied that he would be safe there, we walked the few yards to the car. Rusty was there before us, grinning all over his doggy face.

Puzzled, we inspected the small gate. It was firmly fastened. We repeated the process several times, with the same result. By now I had learned that if I wanted to know what made Rusty tick I had to hide and watch to see what was happening. DW put the dog back in the pen while I lingered in the nearby woodshed. I gasped to see Rusty sailing over that seven-foot fence with the greatest of ease.

In due course we had a chain-link overhang added to the fence top, and that foiled him for a while. However, the next time we tried to go away without him, he once again escaped within minutes. It was back to the woodshed for me. By this time, he realized that he was being watched and he would not try his Houdini act when he suspected I was nearby.

This time, he lay down and got out through the three-inch space underneath the gate. To do this he sucked in his breath while he wriggled through. If I hadn't seen it for myself, I never would have believed it, because he had a large, solid head. I would love to know how he figured this out, but then this was the dog who tried to read books by turning the pages over and putting his nose into the spine. In the end, we had to wedge a rock under the gate, and this solved the problem at last. Never having caught a mouse or a bat in the act, although they have certainly come into the house, I assume that they, too, can manage to suck themselves in when the need arises.

Rusty had worked out his escape route for himself. I have no way of knowing whether smaller mammals possessed similar intelligence, or whether they simply act instinctively. However, raccoons are also capable of independent thought. I recall the day when I went to interview a countrywoman for a book I was researching.

This is her story.

Having been tired the previous evening, she had gone to bed early, leaving her supper dishes unwashed in the kitchen. When she got up in the morning, she found a raccoon sitting on the counter, happily finishing up the leftovers.

How had it got in? A "cat flap" had been installed, so that her pet could go in and out at will, but because our winters are so severe, this opened into a cupboard in her sink unit rather than directly into the kitchen itself. The raccoon had pushed open the flap and gone into the cupboard, and from there managed to gain access to the kitchen. From there it was but a short climb to the counter top, where breakfast awaited.

SQUIRREL TALES

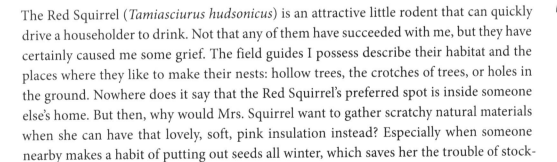

The Red Squirrel (*Tamiasciurus hudsonicus*) is an attractive little rodent that can quickly drive a householder to drink. Not that any of them have succeeded with me, but they have certainly caused me some grief. The field guides I possess describe their habitat and the places where they like to make their nests: hollow trees, the crotches of trees, or holes in the ground. Nowhere does it say that the Red Squirrel's preferred spot is inside someone else's home. But then, why would Mrs. Squirrel want to gather scratchy natural materials when she can have that lovely, soft, pink insulation instead? Especially when someone nearby makes a habit of putting out seeds all winter, which saves her the trouble of stocking her own larder.

At various times, squirrels have attempted to break into the house, but the worst destruction occurred in a small log cabin that has been winterized for use as a guest house. Apart from storage it hasn't been used for that purpose for several years, ever since a big old barn was converted into much larger guest quarters.

The ancient shingles on the cabin were deteriorating and the time came when they had to be replaced with a steel roof. When the shingles were removed, we discovered that squirrels had managed to make an entranceway underneath. Once inside the cabin, they had discovered a very nice couch, which they had apparently fallen on with squeals of joy. They had spent a very comfortable winter curled up in its depths, and the mess they made was indescribable. A man with a strong stomach kindly hauled it away to the dump for me.

As keen birdwatchers, we have always put out feeders in winter, and, of course, the squirrels come to these, racing up to me with chattering teeth, telling me to stand aside so they can get started on the food. They scale the walls of the house to rip down the suet balls, and when there is seed on the ground they rush at the birds to chase them away. There are feeders on the market that are said to baffle squirrels. We have tried them all, but the squirrels can manage each and every one. The latest is a tubular affair with small holes at intervals, equipped with perches for small birds. No squirrel can reach inside those holes, but our neighbourhood Attila knows what to do about that. The squirrel swings back and forth, taking the feeder with it until seeds spill from the holes, and then descends to the ground to mop them up.

I like to watch squirrels feeding. They pick up a seed or a peanut with their mouths, and hold it steady in their tiny paws while they start to eat. When they have something that takes a lot of chewing, they stand up and fold their forelegs across their chests.

One spring, our local pair of squirrels produced three young, which they brought out to explore the feeding area. All of a sudden, a rival family appeared, which caused great indignation on the part of the homegrown group. The adult male (or so I supposed, although for all I know it may have been its mate) got up on its hind legs and faced the intruders. His opposite number did the same. I was amazed when the pair began to spar with their front paws, for all the world like a pair of boxing champs. It wasn't long before this deteriorated into a melee of biting and squealing, but I was delighted to have seen this unusual bit of byplay.

Each autumn, I buy several fifty-pound sacks of sunflower seeds from a local farmer. Not only is this cheaper than buying those expensive little bags of seed at the supermarket, it is also much better quality.

I store these seeds in steel garbage cans, kept for that purpose, and last winter placed them in the cats' porch, which is unheated. It wasn't long before a squirrel sniffed them out and chewed its way through the screens to get inside. Even so, I was confident that it wouldn't be able to get at the seeds. The lids fit so tightly that I often have trouble getting them off. When I looked out one morning, however, I noticed a lid lying on the floor some distance away from the can and the contents had a top layer of discarded shells. The little beast had had a field day. Far from carrying the seeds to a nearby cache, or to hungry young, it had sat there and gorged itself.

I replaced the lid, and for good measure put a cedar log on top. Several nights in a row, I heard a crash coming from the porch as the log was pushed off. The following night, it stayed in place but the bark had been shredded and scattered about. Either the squirrel assumed that

ABOVE LEFT: *A Red Squirrel poses for the camera. These creatures are both beautiful and destructive.*

ABOVE RIGHT: *Like all young creatures, these Red Squirrels are curious to see what the outside world is all about.*

this was the way to get in, or it had other plans for the bark. It is known that squirrels like to line their nests with shredded bark — those who don't find nice, soft insulation, of course!

Poison Ivy Acres is also home to the larger Grey Squirrel (*Sciurus carolinensis),* which we call the Black Squirrel because they appear in their black phase here. Although they seldom come to the house, I sometimes meet them in the woods.

When I was a child in Wales, Red Squirrels were few and far between. After Grey Squirrels had been introduced into the country years ago, these squirrels had taken over to the point where the smaller species was becoming endangered. I understand that they are now recovering, and, like me, some householders are finding their homes invaded by marauding little beasties.

When I was young my mother had a charming book written by a man who had taken a pair of orphaned Red Squirrels into his home. It contained a photo of the little creatures clinging to the curtains, and I can imagine the state the fabric was in before they had been there very long! I wish I could get hold of that book now, to see what became of them. Perhaps they were released into the wild in due course.

A SQUIRREL'S HOARD

All my life I've been led to believe that squirrels stockpile nuts and seeds for the winter. Doesn't everyone else believe that, too? I've heard people say they are "squirreling away money" — putting something aside for a rainy day. In the fall, I stockpile staple foods to be used in the winter months. Potatoes, bags of cat food, and canned goods are too hard to bring in by toboggan, so I know I'm being prudent by preparing in advance.

Some animals are conditioned to make winter caches. The chipmunks strip the Amur Maples bare of seeds, carrying them away in their fat little cheeks. If the coming winter is harsher than usual, they won't have to worry.

Those squirrels, though, are they really as industrious as everyone seems to think? One summer, when it seemed that the countryside was being overrun with the little animals, some people captured them in life traps and drove them away to pastures new. Field naturalists condemn this practice, explaining that it would cause hardship for the squirrels that would have been taken far from their stockpiles of food and thus would have no chance of making a new cache before the bad weather.

Ginger watches with great indignation as a Red Squirrel licks the peanut-butter mixture from the wall. The small rodent seemed to know that it was safe because the cat couldn't reach down that far.

But if my local squirrels are saving up for winter, just where are they keeping the food? As far as I can tell, they eat everything on the spot and keep nothing in reserve. For a while I thought it was squirrels who were knocking down the acorns from the Bur Oaks, but no. A closer look proved that the Blue Jays were the culprits. The squirrels seemed to spend their days chasing each other away from the seeds I threw out, and if they were hoarding some, I certainly didn't see it happening.

In January, they made a lot of little tunnels in the snow, which hardened into ice as the mercury tumbled. They popped in and out of these, seemingly at random. Since they spent all day, from dawn until dusk, filling their bellies, they certainly weren't drawing on any previously stored food.

When shopping for fruit and vegetables, I noticed a large bag of peanuts in the shell, which I bought as a treat for the jays. Naturally, the squirrels came forward for their share, and I saw one little creature carry off a peanut and place it in one of the tunnels.

Aha! I thought. *It is making a cache at last. Possibly the tunnel is the entrance to a winter den.*

This went on for some time, with the squirrel returning for more as long as the peanuts lasted. The entrance to the tunnel must have been full by that time. I was surprised when the squirrel stationed itself at the tunnel and proceeded to work its way through the peanuts, pausing occasionally to scold some passing bird attracted by the nuts. It kept going until all the nuts were gone. When I went out to have a look, the squirrel chattered at me quite furiously although there was nothing left to steal.

I have come to the conclusion that my local squirrels haven't bothered to store food for the winter this year, and why should they, when seeds are thrown out on a daily basis for the birds? What I would like to know is how they figured this out, but I guess it will have to remain a mystery.

FLYING SQUIRRELS

When I stepped outside to give the dogs their "last roundup" before settling in for the night, something small and dark shot past my head. *Surely that wasn't a bat*, I thought. Bats leave here in the middle of October and do not return until mid-April, and this was late February.

Having returned inside, I went upstairs to my office and settled down to watch. Before long, I was rewarded with a sighting of a Northern Flying Squirrel (*Glaucomys sabrinus*). It settled itself in a small bird feeder, which is just below the windowsill, and began to feed. I switched on the outside light to get a better look. It was a small, brown squirrel with a white belly. Its eyes were enormous and round; my grandmother would have called them boot-button eyes. Most attractive little animals, flying squirrels are much smaller than Red Squirrels, and they don't really fly. They have a membrane, or fold of skin, between their front and hind legs, which enables them to glide through the air.

They remain dormant for much of the cold weather but do emerge occasionally. A second squirrel now arrived, and then the first one glided off towards the spruce trees, soon to be followed by the other one. Possibly they were a mating pair, for these creatures come together in late winter and produce their young in April or May, after a forty-day gestation period.

Northern Flying Squirrels. At Poison Ivy Acres, these charming little creatures can be seen gliding from tree to tree at night, oblivious to the glare of the floodlights.

Not all encounters are so peaceful. DW had a brush with an angry mother when he went to clean out some bluebird nesting boxes and found a family of flying squirrels inside. The little rodent had chosen this box in which to bring up her family of four. An unsuspecting DW unscrewed the front of the box and the squirrel flew out at him. It's hard to say which of them had the greater shock. The young mother certainly did her share of gliding on that occasion. As for DW, well, you might say that he promptly glided off!

Years ago, we had a surprise of a different kind when we found that flying squirrels had broken into our attic. Wanting to get all of them out before the hole was filled in, DW set a series of life traps. The surprise came when we captured no fewer than fourteen of the little rascals! Another surprise was their colouring: they were all pale grey rather than the usual brown, more like the Southern Flying Squirrel.

In Anne Innis Dagg's *Mammals of Ontario,* I was intrigued to read an account of how this animal got its scientific name. Apparently *sabrinus* was the term used by the Romans to describe England's Severn River. It was applied to the Northern Flying Squirrel when it was first found and described in the Severn River area of Ontario, which in turn had been named after the British waterway.

THE YEAR OF THE CHIPMUNK

Not long ago, we experienced what I remember as the year of the chipmunk. I don't know how it was in other parts of Ontario, but in our township there was a definite chipmunk boom. They were everywhere! Each time I drove along a township or county road, they were there before me, usually making a suicidal dash in front of the car. There was no hope of avoiding them, and it saddened me to leave those tiny corpses in my wake.

There are many mysteries in nature. I have noticed that certain populations appear to soar at times, while in other years something happens to threaten a particular species. A case in point is the current very worrying demise of bees, which are under attack from mites. Humans are not exempt from pandemics, and, sad to say, it seems that scientists no sooner manage to get one disease under control than some other nasty, hitherto unknown, scourge pops up. Perhaps this is nature's way of population control, yet that thought is unacceptable to us as human beings. It has to be fought, tooth and nail.

Meanwhile, the chipmunk population seemed to have come back to normal, at least at Poison Ivy Acres. For much of the year, the Eastern Chipmunk (*Tamias striatus*) comes close to the house, delighting everyone who sees it. This small member of the squirrel family is quite tame and will often approach us when we are eating outside, hoping for a handout. My mother, visiting here from the old country, was charmed to see a chipmunk nibbling on a piece of macaroni it held in its tiny paws.

Next to the beaver, the chipmunk is one of the hardest workers here. It has pouches inside its cheeks, which it fills with the seeds it finds until it resembles a squirrel with a toothache. The chipmunk carries these seeds away to store for the winter, when it hibernates for much of the cold weather. Sometimes I have seen a chipmunk hiding seeds inside a stone fence, as drystone walls are called in this district.

Last year, I noticed that the chipmunks have become much more aggressive in collecting food. The Amur Maples were stripped bare of seeds in a very short time, whereas many of these previously remained in place throughout the fall.

They were also a nuisance in the garden in the spring and summer. The vegetable garden is surrounded by a chain-link fence, set in a concrete rim, and this keeps most animals out. The chipmunks, however, can squirm through the links, and then the sky is the limit. They remove tomatoes from the vine and leave them lying on the ground after taking only a small bite out of them. They eat the buds off my Shrub Roses and Oriental Poppies, and when there are no more left they cross the yard to tackle the Day Lilies. Why has this been happening in the past two years, when chipmunks have been here forever? Possibly it's a case of "plant it and they will come."

Tame and friendly, the Eastern Chipmunk is a hardworking little animal that sometimes deserves a treat!

Another recent observation of mine is that a few chipmunks seem to be rather smaller than the rest. At first, I thought they must be juveniles, but now I wonder if they are the Least Chipmunk (*Eutamias minimus*), which are also found in Ontario. According to my field guides, the Least Chipmunk has two white stripes on its side, with the stripes extending down to the rump. The Eastern Chipmunk has a white stripe bordered by two black stripes on each side, which stop short of the rump. It also has a dark stripe down its back, and facial stripes above and below the eye. The latter description fits the chipmunks I see around the house, but when spring comes I mean to pay closer attention to those I meet on my walks, in the hope of identifying some of the smaller species.

 # A WILD CAT REMEMBERED

When I heard a big cat screaming in the cedar bush, I was transported back to the scene of one of my most interesting childhood sightings. I was about ten years old, playing at the bottom of the garden where it joined a farmer's field, when I looked up to see an oversized, grey-brown striped cat staring at me from the other side of the fence. It was a long-legged animal, with a jowly, heavy-set face and a large, bushy tail. I'd never seen anything quite like it. Fascinated, I continued to stare back at the beast until it finally gave up and padded away.

Thrilled, I rushed indoors to tell my mother all about it. Busy with her housework, she was not impressed.

"I expect you've seen an ordinary cat, dear. Some tomcats do grow to quite a size."

In vain, I protested that I had seen something quite out of the ordinary. She smiled kindly and carried on with her baking, having no time to waste in idle talk.

Months later our class went on a school trip to the National Museum of Wales, and to my amazement I found my big cat there, mounted on a pedestal. The accompanying information stated that this was a wildcat, once found in Wales, but extinct since the 1880s. (In South Wales, it probably died out at an even earlier date.)

Even at that age I wasn't naive enough to think that a little pocket of these cats had somehow survived in the nearby Black Mountains. However, it was a great puzzle to me, because I knew what I'd seen and it was no ordinary cat, feral or otherwise.

Since then, I've seen photos of Scottish Wildcats (*Felis silvestris grampia*), of which only about four hundred remain in the wild. An effort to conserve this species is being mounted by the Scottish Wildcat Association. Again, they look very much like the big cat I encountered. While it is highly unlikely that my cat padded all the way down from Scotland to South Wales, I suspect that one might have escaped from captivity, possibly from a zoo or a travelling menagerie.

Correspondence with Dr. Peter Howlett, curator of Vertebrates, Biodiversity, and Systematic Biology at the National Museum of Wales has shed further light on the subject. He points out that the Wildcat is only a little larger than a big domestic cat.

"Perhaps the most distinctive feature is the tail; it always looks bushier, blunt-ended and shorter than a domestic cat. The coat has a buff-grey colour with dark brown or black stripes; a domestic cat would be unlikely to have vertical stripes along the length of the body." He goes on to explain that there is only one species of Wildcat. "The Scottish Wildcat is currently treated as a subspecies but many authorities don't think it warrants subspecific status, so it is unlikely that ones from Wales would have been significantly different."

Because wildcats became extinct in Wales long before the museum was established, it is probable that the specimen I saw there had, in fact, been obtained from Scotland for exhibition purposes.

What I find interesting is that in the past few years there have been claims of big-cat sightings at Ammanford, in South Wales, where we were living when I saw my cat all those years ago. These include pumas (known to us in Ontario as cougars and black panthers). This suggests that exotic species have more recently escaped from captivity or been released into the wild.

As we know, a number of big-cat escapees, even lions and tigers, are occasionally seen roaming loose in Ontario. So far, none of those have turned up at Poison Ivy Acres! However, as I relate in my next story, other species have certainly come here!

BIG CATS: A COUGAR ON THE LAWN

I had just gone outside to do some chores when a blood-curdling scream stopped me in my tracks. It was coming from the cedar bush just beyond the sugar shack, and it was obvious that some large animal was there, making its presence felt. Not wanting to take any chances, I retreated to the house in a hurry.

Could it have been a Bobcat (*Lynx rufus*)? Bobcats are not unknown in our area, although they are seldom seen. On hearing my story, a man who cuts timber told me that he had once found a bobcat staring down at him from a high branch in his bush. "Given a chance, they'll spring on you, you know," he advised me.

Some time after this, I found some large cat tracks in the snow. Using my book of animal tracks I tried to decide if these had been made by a bobcat, or possibly a Lynx (*Lynx Canadensis*). Lynx tracks are larger, but otherwise look much the same as bobcat tracks, and, given the fact that paw prints always expand in the snow, and I'm no great expert on animal tracks, I couldn't come to any conclusion. Although rarely seen here, more often frequenting country to the north of us, the lynx is not unknown in these parts, where one is occasionally found by trappers. My property is ideal for these cats, being rich in their favourite food, the Snowshoe Hare, as well as other small mammals and frogs.

I have since learned that a lynx — and possibly the bobcat, too — utters these eerie screams during the mating ritual, and that was probably what I heard. This, of course, means that there was probably a pair of these big cats in my bush, unless of course it was just a solitary beast attempting to attract a mate.

I longed to see any resulting litter of kittens, but it wasn't to be. Perhaps it was just as well, as I wouldn't like to come face to face with a large protective mother cat! However, this is not the end of my big-cat story!

One summer day, going to the bedroom window to shake out a mat, I caught a glimpse of a big, tan-coloured animal loping along through the long grass near the creek. It wasn't moving like a deer and it was lighter in colour. It disappeared out of sight within seconds. Frustrated, I went to my field guides to try to decide what this could be, but again, I couldn't make up my mind. The sighting had been so brief, and I hadn't had time to snatch up my binoculars. As a result the books' descriptions of markings were unhelpful.

Another puzzle was its size. The upper weight for a bobcat is sixty-eight pounds; a lynx is smaller. My dogs weigh up to seventy-five pounds, and they were nothing like the height and length of what I had seen. Being used to seeing them racing about in the same place, I was able to make the comparison in my mind's eye.

Months later, I had a sighting that made up for this disappointment. Glancing out of that same window, I saw a huge, long-tailed cat standing on the edge of the lawn, apparently watching the house. Down below, my house cats were sunning themselves in their screened porch. Were they the big cat's intended prey? Cautiously opening the window to get a better look, I saw the animal lashing its tail as it swivelled its head to look up at me. Moments later it bounded away.

Stunned, I decided that I'd been looking at a Cougar (*Felis concolor*). These animals, also known as Mountain Lions or pumas, can weigh from seventy-five to two-hundred-and-seventy-five pounds. Their territory is Western North America, although occasional sightings have been seen as far east as Canada's Maritime Provinces.

The following week our local newspaper carried an article detailing sightings of a cougar in our area, about thirty miles from my home. One family had to stop their car to let the animal cross the road, while a neighbour saw one on his land while he was cutting wood. The Ministry of Natural Resources received an additional fifteen phone calls from people claiming to have seen a cougar.

A spokesperson stated that cougars usually travel in about a fifty-mile radius, so my visitor may have been the same beast reported in the newspaper. The official went on to say that he receives about six calls a year of cougar sightings. There may be as many as one thousand cougars in captivity in Ontario, and he believes that some sightings may be of animals that have either escaped or been released into the wild.

After reading this report I'm sure that I have sighted a cougar here at least once, although I'm equally sure that the creature making the piercing screams was something different, probably a bobcat. Apparently cougars also scream during the mating season, but as far as I know there has been no report of a mating pair in our area.

Years ago, DW photographed big cats in Kenya — lions, leopards, and cheetahs — and he was delighted to have the chance to see them in the wild. My experience with big cats on our own property may have been less dramatic, but it was thrilling nonetheless.

ONE IN A MILLION: THE STORY OF BLACKIE RYAN

If ever an animal lived life to the full, it was my cat Blackie Ryan. A survivor with a strong personality, he found his way into my heart despite being the terror of the household. When he developed diabetes at the age of sixteen and we had to say goodbye to him, he was sadly missed.

We found him and his three sisters abandoned in a box by the roadside one summer day, when the thermometer had risen to over one hundred degrees. The female kittens were in a bad condition, but he came out of the box in fighting trim, ready to take on the world.

Homes were found for his sisters, but he came to us, walking into the house as if he owned the place.

"Here's a present for you," DW said, handing me a fighting black bundle. All very well for him; he was about to leave for a month in the Arctic and it was left to me to break in a new member of the household. Photographing Polar Bears was a cinch compared to training this feisty little animal.

I named the kitten after Father John Blackwood "Blackie" Ryan, the central figure in Andrew M. Greeley's mystery books. What else could you call a black cat with a small white collar?

Ignored by our two older cats, Smokey and Ginger, Blackie immediately focused on the four dogs, following them everywhere. We kept a supply of miniature bone-shaped biscuits on hand for the purpose of training the younger dogs, and when these were given out it was amusing to see him lining up with the rest, running about with a biscuit clenched in his teeth.

My gentle Irish Setter glanced around in surprise when Blackie first developed the trick of jumping up and swinging from his plumy tail. We thought this was funny until the cat started swinging from the edge of DW's kilt!

When the whistle blew signalling a walk for the dogs, Blackie always wanted to join the throng, but his little legs were too short to keep up with the setters on the trail. Undaunted, he learned to perch on his master's shoulders and, with a paw on each side of DW's head for balance, was able to enjoy a walk of two or three miles without falling.

From then on, the cat knew what was wanted when DW slapped himself on the shoulder, and would leap into action at once. Unfortunately this trick backfired: he grew up thinking it was the right thing to do, and would jump on all and sundry. Visitors had to be warned not to turn their back on the cat. One lady received this news with a scornful look and a curled lip, obviously putting me down as a madwoman. She discovered her mistake when she suddenly found a large animal licking her ear. He had grown into a splendid twenty-pound cat, all muscle, and she wasn't much more than five times his weight!

When I took Blackie for his first annual checkup, the veterinarians were busy and appointments were running late.

"If you have any errands in town, you can leave him here in his carrier while you slip out for a few minutes," the receptionist suggested.

When I returned, I found our usually calm and cheerful vet looking rather shocked. "I took him out of his carrier and he immediately landed on my neck!" he told me.

Blackie Ryan sets out for a hike with his master and the four setters. The cat enjoyed those outings tremendously!

I had to explain that Blackie wasn't going for the jugular. At least, I don't think he was. He deeply resented any interference, and as for getting his temperature taken, well, that was only allowed to happen once!

Clipping his claws was a matter of getting two technicians to subdue him inside a towel while he roared his indignation. On one occasion, other pet owners in the waiting-room looked at each other in dismay at the noise coming from the inner sanctum. As one of the vets laughingly said later, "They must have wondered if we were operating without an anesthetic."

Luckily for him, this feisty behaviour later saved his life. A Great Horned Owl, which, unlike most owls, hunts by day, had a nest near the house with two young owlets to feed. It swooped down on Blackie and tried to carry him off. Fighting and kicking, he managed to escape, and raced back to the protection of the house. Deep gouges on his head and shoulders showed where the bird's talons had grasped him. A few days later a neighbour saw that same bird flying overhead, carrying a fox.

Unlike most cats, Blackie had a very heavy walk, so we always knew when he was coming. He was soon nicknamed "Mr. Thud Thud." I often felt the weight of a heavy paw if I wasn't quick enough filling his dish at meal times. He was also in the habit of slapping any of his housemates who annoyed him. At the same time he could be surprisingly gentle.

Blackie Ryan, aged about eight weeks. Ready for anything!

Clancy, my little grey cat, came to us as a terrified kitten. While she was soon accepted by the other pets, it was Blackie who took her under his wing. One day, hearing strange noises coming from the bathroom, I found him demonstrating how to unroll the toilet paper. His big paw went into action, then he stood back, watching her out of large, round eyes. This was repeated several times until she finally came forward and managed to do what he wanted. Talk about a copycat!

During Blackie's last illness the pair of them used to lie side by side on the bed, the perfect companions. Although he was a cat with a loud voice, he seldom purred, but when Clancy was nearby a soft, contented rumble could be heard.

At the time I had four other dearly loved cats, including twenty-one-year-old Smokey, but there will never be another Blackie Ryan, a cat in a million.

MY FRIEND CLANCY

One Saturday morning in July, I decided to take the household rubbish to the township dump. With Rusty sitting happily in the back seat, I set off without a care in the world. The first thing I saw when I drove through the gate was a tiny grey kitten, standing timidly beside the custodian.

"Is that your kitten?" I asked, pretty sure that it wasn't.

"No, no. I found it here when I arrived to open up," he replied. "I guess somebody left it here last time, when my back was turned."

That had been on the previous Wednesday. Some evil person had left this tiny, helpless creature, barely weaned, out there to starve. It particularly infuriated me to think that this cruel owner had abandoned the little thing on a rubbish dump, showing no respect for life.

I headed for home, meaning to return with some cat food, which would solve the immediate problem. I already had seven pets — four big dogs and three adult cats — how could I make room for more? But I returned, and before I knew it, I had scooped up the kitten and placed it on the floor by the passenger seat.

"What do you think, Rusty?" I asked. The dog peered over the seat, sniffing. Then he looked at me with his big doggy grin and wagged his tail.

"It's fine by me," he seemed to be saying.

On the way home I tried to come up with a name. For some reason, Clancy seemed to fit. Some weeks later I had a visitor from Ireland who asked why I'd given that name to a cat.

It transpired that each of his grandmothers had been a Miss Clancy prior to marriage. I was lost for an explanation.

Once home and in the kitchen, I put the kitten on the floor. On seeing Smokey, a look-alike grey feline and, at that time, my only female cat, Clancy ran to her with a glad cry, only to be cruelly rebuffed with swearing and spitting. Dismayed, the kitten fell back. Having just been taken from her mother, it was obvious that she was desperate for acceptance. There were other cats in the room, but she chose the only other female. How could she have been aware of this? Smokey was neutered and had never had a litter.

Clancy's poor little stomach was completely flat. When I put my hand over her back I could touch my forefinger to my thumb over her abdomen. I opened a can of beef chunks in gravy and put a little on a plate. She gulped it down and was immediately sick.

That first night I put her out in the porch, with a comfortable bed and a litter box. Not knowing if she was house-trained, or whether she would come to harm from the other animals, I felt that was for the best. But when I looked out at locking-up time I saw a pitiful sight. She was sitting on a table with her head thrown back and her eyes closed. From her open mouth came a pitiful soft wail, which broke my heart. The poor beast had been wrenched from her mother, abandoned in the open for three days with all the fearsome noises of the night, and now, for all she knew, it was happening again. How was she to tell the difference?

I picked her up and took her to bed with me. She immediately crawled into my armpit, where she stayed until morning. I must say that I have spent more comfortable nights!

Two days later she began to cough. Before long she was very ill indeed. Although antibiotics were prescribed, I was warned that she probably wouldn't survive. Still angry over the way she'd been treated, I vowed that she should have her chance. The antibiotics didn't work and a second type was prescribed. As she struggled for breath in the night, I held her upright to help her breathe. She snuggled close to me, her eyes filled with suffering. Once again a different antibiotic was prescribed, and the tide began to turn at last. She began to eat the small meals provided for her, and she took an interest in the toys that belonged to the other cats.

Funnily enough, her champion in those early days was my big bruiser of a cat, Blackie Ryan. Was it possible that he remembered his own early days, when he was abandoned in a box by the roadside before we adopted him? I'm not at all sure that cats are capable of putting two and two together in such a manner, even though I do believe that they can communicate with one another in ways we can't begin to fathom. Perhaps it had something to do with his being the odd man out. When he came to us he was rejected by the two senior cats, Smokey and Ginger, who were litter mates. Now he had a little female chum of his own.

Blackie Ryan was a big and powerful cat. His wicked claws wreaked havoc around the house because he refused to let me clip them. The walls and doors bear witness to his efforts to keep them sharp. Any member of the household who annoyed him, whether man or beast, received a clout from a heavy paw, accompanied by a growl of indignation. But he was always as gentle as a lamb with Clancy.

He died some years ago, aged sixteen, and is much missed. Clancy is now thirteen, a patient, dainty little cat, as sweet-natured as they come. A year ago she was diagnosed with diabetes, and she has to have insulin shots twice a day. Not only does she accept these with equanimity, she also knows when the next dose is due, and comes to sit beside me, waiting for it. On the rare occasions when I oversleep, I awake to feel a soft paw patting me on the cheek. Time for breakfast, and that needle.

She is a darling little companion, often sitting on the printer or lying beside me when I'm working at the computer. An indoor cat, she loves to sit on the windowsill, doing a spot of birdwatching. I've been well repaid for bringing her home to live with us.

THE BUNGEE JUMPERS

One sunny day, I was walking the dogs in the hidden field when I witnessed a sight that made me laugh out loud. Two-thirds of the way up a tall tree, a pair of porcupines were engaged in what I can only describe as bungee jumping. One was edging carefully along a narrow branch, while the other was just stepping onto the same fork.

The branch began to sway as they got farther from the main trunk, but this didn't deter them. Soon the branch was moving up and down so that it almost touched the ground before springing back into the air again, but they kept their cool. I doubt if they were performing this exercise for fun! Could it have been some bizarre form of courtship ritual? It certainly seemed as if the second beast was trying to catch up with the first one. They were still at it when I reached the edge of the field, seemingly totally oblivious to me. The dogs hadn't noticed them, so there was nothing to frighten the spiny pair.

Here at Poison Ivy Acres, the North American Porcupines (*Erethizon dorsatum*) are all too plentiful, and I'm sorry to say that at times they've had to be dispatched. One beast actually managed to chomp on an aluminum boat. As if this wasn't bad enough, one started chewing on our log house! It had to go.

"Never shoot a porcupine," one old fellow told us. "Get rid of one, and they'll come over the hill in droves!"

When I was a child in Wales, we often found hedgehogs in our garden. My mother showed me how to pick up the little creatures that had lovely soft fur on the underbelly. When I came to Canada and met my first porcupine, I quickly decided that these giant look-alikes were less user-friendly! That is to say: never walk across your lawn barefoot if a porcupine has been there before you! Some people will tell you that the best way to remove a quill is to snip off the end, which will relieve the pressure inside, allowing you to take out the quill with ease. This is a complete fallacy, which I learned the hard way.

Most of our dogs discovered that it was best not to meddle with a porcupine. When it was a case of one or two quills in the nose, I was able to remove them with pliers, which must have been a painful operation. After removing quills from my own foot, I know how it feels. After coming to me with a woebegone look on their faces, most of the dogs seemed to understand that this unpleasant operation was the only way that order could be restored.

Rusty, however, was a different proposition. He never seemed to learn. Always aggressive with certain animals who trespassed on his territory, he usually ended up with a face full of quills as well as a fair number stuck in other parts of his anatomy. There was no help for it: a trip to the vet was always called for, trips that were to be repeated several times.

"You again!" the vet would say, preparing to insert the needle into Rusty's paw, to administer the anesthetic. After the first couple of times, the dog would hold out his paw for the injection! DW used to joke about it, saying that perhaps he liked the sensation of getting high on the medication. Or perhaps he was like a patient with a toothache, sitting in the dentist's chair, thinking, *let's get this over with*.

Porcupine quills that are left *in situ* can travel all through the body. This is not a myth. Our vet told us that he had once operated on a dog — or was it a post mortem, perhaps? — that was full of quills internally. Not a happy thought.

 # FUR GALORE

Over the years I've had an ermine in my office, a mink on the windowsill, and a muskrat on the lawn — and before anyone tracks me down to complain, I hasten to say that

I'm totally against the idea of trapping animals so that humans can drape themselves in fur coats.

When I had a Girl Guide company I made a habit of tying in this thought with the sixth Guide Law: "A Guide is kind to animals." As a result, one of the girls was highly indignant when she saw me sporting a new camel-hair coat.

"Captain, how could you? After all you've said!"

"No, Andrea, the camel did not have to die in order for me to get this coat."

"Oh! Are you sure?"

All the small animals I have just mentioned were still wearing their own fur coats when they entered my life. The ermine was in the very room where I'm sitting at the computer to write this now. I was typing away when, out of the corner of my eye, I caught a glimpse of something white, just going under the bookcase. When it re-emerged I was most surprised to find a very fine specimen of the weasel family (*Mustela erminea*) staring up at me.

Alerted by me, my husband came running with the camera, and then the chase was on. The ermine declined to be photographed. DW had the easy part; all he had to do was focus the camera, while my job was to herd the creature in the right direction. Well, you try to organize a nimble little creature with evil teeth! I didn't know we had so many places in the house where an animal could hide.

We also had to keep the cats and dogs downstairs so they wouldn't come into contact with this fierce little animal, which, if cornered, was capable of inflicting severe damage on any of them. Finally we gave up the struggle and retreated, leaving a bedroom window open. With great presence of mind, I sprinkled talcum powder on the sill, hoping that a trail of small footprints would let us know when the ermine had made its exit.

The burning question was, how did the animal get into the house in the first place? I suspect that Rusty, our Gordon Setter, was the culprit. He could open any door or window in the house, but he had never learned the knack of closing them after himself. Why the ermine would choose to enter a house filled with four dogs and three cats, I can't imagine, but its arrival was certainly a delightful experience for the humans living there.

While visiting the National Museum of Wales as a child, I was interested to see the robes worn by the Prince of Wales (later to become King Edward VIII) when he was presented to the people of Wales at Caernarfon. They were adorned by a number of snowy white, black-tipped ermine tails. We were told that, historically, ermine tails have been used to trim royal garments. Personally, I would rather see these tails where they belong: attached to a living ermine.

A mink peers into the conservatory. Blue soon spotted the intruder and sounded the alarm, but the mink was not perturbed.

I don't know what the mink had in mind, either, when it hopped up on the outside sill of the living room window. It stood there, peering in, for quite a long time. The cats sat on the other side of the glass with their tails lashing. Might our visitor have had a good meal in mind when it saw the cats? The American Mink (*Mustela vison*) does enjoy devouring small mammals, and it will prey on rabbits, among other things. This sighting, too, was a fine experience for us, as we were able to get a good look at the mink, face to face, something that surely doesn't happen to many people.

The pond below the house is occasionally visited by Common Muskrats (*Ondatra zibethicus*) and North American Beavers (*Castor canadensis*) and it's interesting to see them disporting themselves in the water. At one time we had trout in this pond, which meant that it was very popular with the neighbouring herons and Ospreys. DW received a thorough scolding from a muskrat when he attempted to catch us a fish supper, despite the fact that these rodents are not fish eaters. They do enjoy frogs and crayfish, which are found in the nearby creek.

My most favourite visitors of all are the Northern River Otters (*Lutra canadensis*). They live at the edge of a big pond a long way from the house. I seldom go there these days because the forest is now so dense that one could easily get lost. But the otters know the way to the smaller pond here.

One summer evening, I looked outside to see a pair of otters having a lovely time. They were sliding down the bank into the water. I could almost imagine them shouting, "Whee, here we go!" They were turning somersaults over and over again, and I felt fortunate to be able to watch their antics. I crept closer and closer, but they didn't seem to mind.

The world of nature is a wonderful one, and I'm delighted to be able to share my home with so many of its species.

FACE TO FACE WITH A FISHER

One summer day I was walking along the trail overlooking the creek when I was startled by a dark animal that rushed across my path, tail outstretched, before disappearing into the undergrowth. In the heat of the moment I thought it was a cat, until I realized that the animal was dark brown in colour, quite unlike any cat likely to appear in these parts. After some thought I finally decided that it had to have been a fisher. Since then I've seen many more of them and have been able to get a much closer look.

The Fisher (*Martes pennanti*) was first described by the Welsh naturalist Thomas Pennant in the eighteenth century. It is a member of the Family *Mustelidae*, which includes the mink, the weasels, the Pine Marten, and the wolverine. For many years the fisher was trapped for its fur and it came close to extinction. Following intervention by the Ministry of Natural Resources, the species has increased and is now in a healthy state.

Fishers can be vicious, and no small animal is safe from their clutches. They can swim, run fast, and climb trees. They are the only predators that can take down a porcupine by going for the soft underbelly. On several occasions, I've met one on my lane. Usually they run away, but one morning I was faced with a particularly large one, probably a male. We stared at each other for a long moment before it turned and ran away. I don't know what might have been on its mind, but evidently it decided I was too large to tackle, and for that I was thankful!

When experiencing the results of a fisher's hunting forays I have to remind myself that it is a carnivore, programmed by nature to eat meat, although it also eats berries and nuts. However, when every cat in the neighbourhood was wiped out by fishers one summer, this was hard to take. Fortunately, my own cats were safely indoors, having been transformed into indoor pets following Blackie Ryan's escape from the Great Horned Owl. Poor Merlin was not so lucky.

Merlin, a handsome grey tabby with a white-shirt front and paws, turned up at the house one winter day. I first saw him crouching under a spruce tree, watching the kitchen window, but when I went outside he ran off. This was repeated for several days, until he eventually came to investigate a kibble-filled dish I had left outside for him.

My cats are fed twice a day, and Merlin (as I named him) came to know our routine. When my cats were lined up at the kitchen counter, Merlin would be waiting at the back door, running off as soon as the door was opened. He wouldn't approach the food while I was there, preferring to keep a wary eye on me from a distance. I made a bed for him in the open-sided woodshed, hopeful that in time he could be tamed. Then would come the task of bringing him indoors and introducing him to the other animals.

Alas, one morning I noticed fisher tracks all around the yard and buildings. There was little I could do to protect the cat, but I surmised that his days were numbered. I had to go into town that afternoon, and when I returned at feeding time there was no sign of Merlin. I searched for any sign of him, called in vain, and then put out his food in the usual place. The dish was still full the next morning. The poor cat was never seen again, nor were there any paw prints in the snow.

Since then I have heard many stories about fishers and their hunting exploits. One family watched in horror as a fisher climbed a hollow tree where a family of raccoons had made a home. Showing no mercy, it picked off the kits one by one.

Fishers will travel over a wide range in their search for food. Hard though it is to watch such happenings, we must accept that their survival depends on this.

 ## MAKE WAY FOR THE GROUNDHOG

My mother was born on Candlemas Day, a feast that is also dedicated to St. Brigid of Ireland. In Canada, of course, the second of February is also known as Groundhog Day and I loved to tease her by phoning to wish her a happy Groundhog Day. An old rhyme says that if the weather is fine on this day, there will be six more weeks of winter. In Canada, this piece of folklore has been adapted to say that if the groundhog leaves its burrow and can see its shadow, there will be six more weeks of winter to come.

Various parts of the country have adopted groundhogs, which are brought out of hibernation on February 2 to see if they can predict the duration of winter, a harmless superstition that lends a little amusement in the harsh days of winter. The most famous is Wiarton Willie, of Wiarton, in Ontario's Bruce Peninsula. When the original Willie died in 1999 at the age of twenty-two, the news made headlines across the country. Another famous forecaster in the United States is Punxsutawney Phil, a groundhog in Punxsutawney, Pennsylvania.

Here in the country everyone knows the Groundhog (*Marmota monax*). A member of the Family *Sciuridae,* Order *Rodentia,* it is also known as a woodchuck, a name derived from the Cree language. They can be seen in country fields and on rural roads, and when danger threatens they will even climb a tree, if they are unable to reach the safety of their burrows.

I have to admit that they are not my favourite animals. Perhaps I'd feel differently if the ones on my property had some useful attributes like Wiarton Willie! However, their behaviour is quite the reverse. When they chop the heads off the French Marigolds it's particularly maddening, because the flowers are there to deter other pests from attacking the tomatoes. Similarly, it's infuriating to catch a groundhog in the act of standing on its hind legs, rooting through a tub which has been freshly planted with Morning Glory seeds.

Of course, when that happens I let out a screech and chase them away, but they don't seem to get the message. Instead, they chatter at me to express their annoyance. I suppose they feel that a good feast is worth the risk of being found by me. A particularly large groundhog always seems to hang around outside the house each spring. I suspect that this is an expectant mother because one year the animal was waddling along with its belly almost touching the ground. Either that, or it was an obese male who'd had a wonderful feast among the vegetables. But I decided that this is hardly likely because groundhogs are quite skinny when they emerge from hibernation and it takes time for them to recover their body weight.

The tunnels they dig can be downright dangerous. Once, when walking across a field, I stepped into one of their holes, hidden by the long grass, and fell down. This wouldn't have mattered, apart from the fact that I fell sideways, but with my boot caught in the hole, still going ahead, as it were, and my knee received a painful wrench.

The dogs, who treat most wildlife with respect, have been known to kill any groundhog that crosses their path. Although I prefer to avoid this, it doesn't always work out that way and then I have to dispose of the corpse.

I've always thought that groundhogs aren't the brightest of creatures, but a certain episode made me realize that they are capable of reasoning — at least where their survival is at stake. I was walking along, lost in thought, when I suddenly looked up and found that the four dogs and I were standing in a ring, with a groundhog crouching in the middle. Blue was pointing at the intruder, and the other setters were honouring his point.

It was only a matter of time before the carnage began, and the trapped animal knew it. Its eyes flickered from one dog to another and then it charged. I was the one chosen for the assault; it seemed to know that among the five of us, I alone did not pose a threat. And it was right. I hastily stepped out of its path. In a flash the groundhog had disappeared down its hole and the dogs were right there, wagging their tails and scrabbling uselessly at the entrance. How's that for a good survival tactic?

Not far from the kitchen door there is a wooden ramp, shaped something like a table with a sloping top. It was built to help the older dogs get into the SUV when they were no longer able to leap up by themselves. This year, a groundhog has dug a tunnel underneath it, which was a smart move. It is surrounded by Crown Vetch, a plant that the creature seems to enjoy eating, and on warm evenings she comes out to sit atop the wooden structure for a breath of air while, presumably, her young ones are safely tucked up in the nursery below.

Some naturalists maintain that groundhogs are stupid creatures, but after my experiences I can no longer agree with them.

SKUNKED!

I was coming down the lane after an evening walk when I noticed a skunk in the distance, right in the middle of the path. I paused, considering my options. The skunk had the same idea. It rose on its hind legs and stared fixedly in my direction. I had to laugh. Talk about the gunfight at the O.K. Corral! We looked like two characters in an old Western movie, ready to have a shoot-out.

I concluded that perhaps the skunk had young hidden nearby. They like to make their dens near water, and this animal was standing near a culvert through which water was running from the higher ground in the hardwood bush, down to the pond below the house. Other than crossing over the culvert there was no way for me to get home, so I took a few tentative steps forward. Alarmed, the skunk dived into the undergrowth, never to be seen again. With a sigh of relief, I pressed on. I have tangled with a skunk in the past and have no wish to repeat the experience.

Our dog, Rusty, had one bad fault, and we were never able to cure him of it. Although he was friendly with people, he couldn't bear it if his territory was invaded by a strange dog or a wild animal. He was a dreadful fighter, which was how I came to learn more about skunks.

The Striped Skunk (*Mephitis mephitis*) is a pretty black-and-white animal, about the size of a domestic cat. Its method of defence is to let fly with a stream of evil-smelling liquid. When a dog gets "skunked," a large amount of tomato juice is needed to neutralize the smell, although veterinarians now say that a mixture of vinegar and water can work just as well, at less expense.

Well, I took the dogs for a walk in the hardwood bush, which they loved because a large field lay beyond it where they could gallop to their hearts' content. Then we met a skunk. The other setters stayed well back, pointing, but Rusty was furious. The skunk lifted its tail and the dog received a stinging eyeful of noxious liquid, which, far from causing him to retreat with his tail between his legs, caused him to lunge at the skunk in fury.

In Canada, skunks are among the worst carriers of rabies, and, although this one looked quite healthy, I couldn't take a chance. As the dog lunged again, I stepped forward to grab him by the collar, assuming that the skunk had done its worst. I now know that skunks always keep something in reserve! We headed for home, with me attempting to hold my breath. Rusty, by now firmly controlled by a leash, kept peering back over his shoulder, ready to have another go.

All my clothes went straight into the washing machine; this was one occasion when the bedroom door remained firmly shut. I didn't want the bedding to be contaminated by that dog! A call to the vet reassured me that even if the skunk had been ill — which I was sure wasn't the case — the dogs would have been all right because their rabies vaccinations were up to date.

"This dog would make a good mascot for your old regiment," I told DW, a veteran of the Normandy campaign in the Second World War.

"I don't know what you mean," he said.

"Well, remember their motto," I replied. He laughed.

The proud motto of the Canadian Scottish Regiment is *Deas Gu Cath* — Ready for the Fray. It describes Rusty to a tee.

LIFE IN THE "EVIL BAT HOUSE"

Back in the 1820s, a section of eastern Ontario was known as the Bathurst District. It consisted of what later became the counties of Lanark and Carleton and part of Renfrew. It was named in honour of Henry, the third Earl of Bathurst, who was secretary of state for war and the colonies. Some of my work deals with chain migrations of people from Scotland and Ireland who settled in Lanark and Renfrew, and I know that certain correspondence in the Colonial Office papers regarding the settlements was addressed to this man, or responded to by him.

Recently, a friend who has been researching another aspect of these settlements found an interesting reference in a paper that was prepared by an American man who is a descendant of one of these Scottish settlers. His ancestor, he said, had immigrated to Canada "sponsored by a man called Ervil Bathouse." Obviously, the writer had never heard of the Earl of Bathurst!

To me this malapropism was just one step away from "Evil Bat House," reminding me as it did of the most unhappy summer when I lived in one! Bats have lived in our district for a long time. They spend the winter in a disused mine at Mount St. Patrick, twelve miles by road from Poison Ivy Acres, possibly less as the bat flies. In summer, they spread out across the district, looking for places where they can roost by day, coming out at night to feed on the mosquito population. Most of those who come here are Little Brown Bats, with a smaller population of Grey Bats.

Just as many birds do, the bats migrate by night. I once had the privilege of hearing and seeing them arrive in an enormous cloud, twittering as they came. They used to roost in the old, open drive shed, which I really didn't mind. Bats are fascinating little creatures with much to recommend them — so long as they stay in their rightful place, which I consider to be out-of-doors!

However, what I remember as the Summer of the Bat was a different kettle of fish. Dozens of Little Brown Bats managed to get into my house, causing a great amount of stress to humans and animals alike. Many of them came down the chimney and into the living-room fireplace. Others managed to squeeze in through the small holes where heating and water pipes entered the house. Some entered via the hot air vents leading out from the stove and the clothes dryer. Many more, who didn't get inside, took up residence behind the caps covering the outdoor electrical sockets.

Why has this happened? I wondered. We were having an unusually hot summer, and, according to a bat book I read in desperation, female bats look for cooler places to use as a nursery. But surely this wasn't the whole story? Bats arrive in April when the weather has not yet had a chance to heat up. A horrid thought occurred to me.

At Christmas, I had received a new dog whistle, a high-frequency pipe that could be heard by animals but not by humans. I had used it with enthusiasm, especially when the dogs went out to relieve themselves before settling down for the night. Bats communicate with each other at high frequencies. Was it possible that they had tuned in to this tiny gadget, somehow interpreting the message as an invitation to move in for the summer?

Laugh at that suggestion if you wish. The fact remained that a whole horde of bats had invaded my territory, and I wanted them out. Bats can carry rabies. Their droppings can carry infections. I stood in the middle of my living room with dozens of bats flitting around my head, looking like a medieval illustration of St. Francis of Assisi. Knowing that it would be costly to bring in an exterminator from the city, I made the phone call anyway. "Can't be done. We're not allowed to use that pesticide any more. It's toxic to humans. Sorry!" The next man said vaguely that he thought bats were protected creatures and he didn't want trouble with the law.

I tried to contact some scientist or bat expert who might be able to advise me. *Perhaps they can capture the bats in a humane way?* I thought. Unfortunately, the internet hadn't yet come into play, and all my efforts failed. I next went to the nearest town, hoping to buy a butterfly net that might do the trick, but there were none to be found. I went home and tried a fishing net, but the holes were too big and the bats flew straight through them.

As a rule, I don't believe in harming wildlife, and I'm sure that bat enthusiasts will be highly indignant to read about what happened next, but under the circumstances I felt that there was no choice. Two friends came over after dark, bringing their tennis racquets with them. Using a technique worthy of Wimbledon they downed as many bats as possible, leaving me to scoop the stunned creatures into a pail, to be released outside.

Rusty watched us with interest, and the following evening he leapt into action, bringing down one bat after another. Unfortunately, the bats took evasive action, hiding themselves behind the many framed pictures on the walls and clinging to the back of the curtains. One even went inside the spout of the electric kettle. I had to take all these furnishings into another room, where they remained for the summer. That wasn't the only thing that was banished. I couldn't let visitors into the house — not that they were keen to come inside, once they'd heard my sad story.

I read *Just Bats*, an excellent book by the noted bat expert, M. Brock Fenton. The book recommended keeping the lights on in the house to discourage bats from entering. This I did. On the theory that what comes in, may go out, a friend suggested leaving all the doors and windows open. I decided against that. It sounded like an invitation to wildlife, more insects, and still more bats. I did leave the patio door open and several bats moved out to the porch, where they arranged themselves on the screens. In the morning, I closed the inner door and opened the screen door, and a few departed the next night.

Meanwhile, I was able to observe the bats on the screens. They are so small and defenceless-looking when their wings are folded. They spent the time grooming themselves with one leg. Having believed that bats hang upside down at all times, I was surprised to see them the other way up when they were doing this.

Only one bat came upstairs. I was about to drop off to sleep when something whirred past my head. I decided that it must have come under the bedroom door, where there is a space about an inch high. After that, I blocked it off with a towel. Each time I came down in the morning I saw bats clinging to the walls, like so many dark blobs. Unfortunately for me, the upstairs ceilings and sloping walls are covered with pine board and batten, beautiful woodwork which shows a good many dark, blobbish knot marks. In the moonlight, it appeared as if the invaders had come upstairs, and I didn't sleep well for weeks.

As usual, the bats left in mid-October. Workmen were called in to seal any small cracks that were visible in the log walls or ceiling beams. I was unable to find any accumulation of droppings either inside the house or outside, which would have signalled a place of entry, but I wasn't prepared to take chances.

When April came I was filled with trepidation, but the bat incident wasn't repeated. I read the bat book again. The author tells the story of a man in Zimbabwe who discovered that some bats were greatly attracted to the skirl of his bagpipes. Suddenly, light dawned. The previous spring, I had been given some records of bagpipe music and I'd played these with enthusiasm, with the outside speakers turned on. Had the bats heard this, and accepted the invitation to visit the house? Believe me, much as I enjoy the sound of the pipes, I haven't played those records since! Was the problem caused by the record or the whistle? Without proof, I really don't know.

WEASELS AT A GLANCE

I was driving up the hill towards the gate one summer morning when I had to stop for a family of brown-coloured weasels that were crossing the lane. The mother, as I judged her to be, was quite tiny, and her five youngsters were even smaller. Because they were so much smaller than other weasels I've seen around, I guessed that they must be Least Weasels (*Mustela rixosa*). In her book, *Mammals of Ontario*, Ann Innis Dagg explains that this rare weasel is the smallest carnivore known.

I was delighted to have seen this species for the first time, particularly since they feed on mice, shrews, and insects, and are no threat to birds. Anyone who keeps poultry will well understand the distress I felt, years ago, on viewing the carnage in my hen house after a weasel had been at work.

Last summer, when I was walking down to the house from the woodshed after putting the lawn mower away, a much larger brown weasel crossed my path. As is so often the case in my encounters with wild animals, we stopped to look at each other for a long moment, and then it sidled into a patch of crown vetch and wasn't seen again. Although there are ermines here, otherwise known as the Short-tailed Weasel (*Mustela erminea*), I don't think that it was one of that species in its brown summer coat. The tail of this animal was longer and bushier, leading me to think that it might be the Long-tailed Weasel (*Mustela frenata*). No doubt it was a member of the family that had been the nemesis of my poor hens. I don't keep hens now, but there are plenty of Snowshoe Hares on our property to provide food for carnivores.

Having read up on the life and times of weasels in my *The Audubon Society Field Guide to North American Mammals*, I have learned that weasels of all types in northern climes turn white in winter, and that this colour change is genetically determined. For example, if a northern weasel is taken south in captivity it still turns white in winter, and a southern weasel taken north remains brown. I haven't yet had the opportunity of checking out all of these colour changes, apart from the ermine. Those particular weasels sometimes come near the bird feeders at night, when small rodents emerge to search for scattered seeds.

I should like to see the Least Weasels again, but I may not get the chance. For one thing, this creature is primarily nocturnal. For another, in common with the other weasels, it can be preyed upon by owls, hawks, and foxes, all of which share their habitat at Poison Ivy Acres, leaving few weasels about the place for me to observe.

All in all, I feel most fortunate to have caught a glimpse of those little weasels when they went out walking that day. It is a chance which may not come again.

 LIFE AT THE CREEK

When I look out on summer evenings, I often see a beaver swimming in the pond below the house. These animals seem so peaceful as they move about, with their noses just above water. There is a lesson to be learned from them. Beavers work so hard, and they deserve time to play. Watching the beaver, I realize that all of us need a break from work and the stresses of everyday life.

Sometimes I stroll down to the pond to have a closer look, and when the beaver sees me coming it gives a loud slap on the water with its big, flat tail. This alarm signal echoes around the valley, warning other beavers of possible danger.

At times, I have found dams on the creek, as well as a lodge and food stockpile. These disappear from time to time in the spring flood, often caused by the removal of dams on other properties. In other places, the beaver's industrious work sometimes leads to trouble and then the animal is classed as a nuisance beaver and trapped out.

Two years ago, I was talking to a friend in the supermarket and we parted company with the shared expectation that both of us would reach home within the hour. I reached home safely, but she found the highway flooded before she came to her hamlet and was unable to go ahead. A dam had burst on private property, causing widespread damage and, of course, the beavers were highly unpopular.

I can only marvel at the amount of work the beavers do. They completely altered the appearance of the beaver meadow at Poison Ivy Acres when they chopped down numerous poplars and swamp willows a few years ago. They then moved upstream and took down larger trees, which they slid down a steep bank to reach the water's edge. From there, they floated the logs to their lodge. There are so many of those weed-like trees on the property that they are welcome to them, but when they started coming farther inland, I wasn't so sure.

Overnight they made their way up the lane and removed some birches there. I thought it must have been an apprentice beaver at work, because those fallen trees remained where they were, beside a tiny pond. This fills with the spring runoff, and the water goes through a culvert under the lane, ending up in the larger pond via a pretty little waterfall. It dries

up in summer, so there is no way to float the logs down to the creek. Balked by this, the beavers then turned to some enormous hardwood trees near the pond itself. Unfortunately, these became hung up against some maples, so again the beaver was thwarted. I was worried about a fine stand of tamaracks and a few nice cedars, but apparently the beavers didn't fancy them, for they are still standing.

There is something inside that hole! Jordie and Blue scent something interesting at the creek.

The dogs were once delighted to find a beaver scent mound on the edge of the beaver meadow. This was a low mound made from a mixture of mud, grass, and sticks, probably impregnated with the scent from the animal's anal glands. This is believed to be a method of marking the beaver's family territory. There was a lot of sniffing and pawing going on; Rusty was especially thrilled. I couldn't smell anything in particular, but, on the other hand,

I am an expert at smelling beaver scat, which has a very distinctive odour. I know this from having to shampoo dogs who have rolled in it!

For centuries beavers have been trapped for their pelts. When I was a child in Wales, it was our habit to wear the national costume on St. David's Day, including the tall black hat. One or two of the girls had real beaver hats, which were family heirlooms. It was likely that these had been made from Canadian beaver, exported by the Hudson's Bay Company at a time when such hats were worn throughout the British Isles. Trapping is not allowed on Poison Ivy Acres, but the beavers here are still at risk from predators, most of which also live on and around the creek. These include foxes, coyotes, otters, and bobcats. Mink are preyed on by foxes and Great Horned Owls, and in turn the mink preys on muskrats, as raccoons have been known to do.

Partly because of their industrious lifestyle, beavers are looked upon as an emblem of Canada and, at present, they are imprinted on the reverse of the five-cent coin. Back in the early 1960s, when the search was on for a new Canadian flag, it was suggested that Canada's furry symbol of hard work, the beaver, should appear on that as well. The powers-that-be rejected this idea, on the grounds that it was inappropriate to depict a member of the rat family on our nation's flag.

ON RACCOONS:

Calling Clooney

One May morning, I looked out of the bedroom window to see a small raccoon staring up at me from the grass below. Raccoons (*Procyon lotor*) are attractive little creatures with their ringed tails and black eye-masks. They can also be a bit of a nuisance to householders, even in urban areas, because they upset garbage cans while foraging for food, and they have also been known to invade attics or chimneys in their search for winter quarters.

We have never had a problem here. There are plenty of hollow logs and trees for them to choose from when they want to den up, and in all but the driest summers our property abounds with berries, grasshoppers, and crayfish, which are all part of their staple diet. But the previous summer, there had been a drought. Nothing had grown properly, and the creek had dried up. This poor little raccoon looked so scrawny that I wondered if she was starving.

I knew I had to be cautious. Raccoons are usually nocturnal, or so I had been led to believe, and this was in broad daylight. Also, raccoons can become rabid, and when wild creatures approach farm buildings, it can be a bad sign. So I threw down some bread crusts from the bedroom window, and the raccoon pounced on them at once, holding one in both of her hands while she ate. (I suppose that paws would be a more accurate term, but raccoons have long, jointed fingers, rather like human hands, and their tracks, when seen in mud or snow, resemble a baby's hand. They pick things up by bringing both "hands" together to scoop up the desired object. If you have seen a toddler picking up food with a spoon in one hand and using the fingers of the other to push the food in the right direction, you'll get the picture. The difference is that the raccoon is far more delicate and efficient at the task than a baby!) Little did I know it at the time, but I would be throwing food out of that window for years to come!

When the raccoon had finished eating she lay down beside the lilacs and surveyed the scene. At that point I had no way of knowing whether the little creature was, in fact, female,

This is Clooney when she first came to the house. Unbeknown to the author, the little animal had five kits hidden nearby.

75

yet she was so small and dainty, about the size of my ten-pound cat, that I began referring to her as "she." Adult raccoons usually achieve a weight of between twelve and thirty pounds.

I gave her the name of Clooney. In the days that followed, she seemed to recognize her name, because she emerged from the shelter of the trees whenever I called her. There is a popular belief that raccoons wash their food before eating it, and indeed this is reflected in their scientific name, *Procyon lotor*. (*Raccoon* derives from a Native word.) However, even though there is a pond within sight of the house, neither Clooney nor the other raccoons who were yet to come were ever seen to do this. She accepted whatever was given to her, and ate it at once.

One evening, when I looked out, she was there as usual, standing on her hind legs, waiting. Her fingers were joined together in an attitude of supplication. Beside her there was a smaller edition of herself. Now I understood. This baby had been sheltering under the deck and was only now allowed out. That was why Clooney had lingered nearby. I was pretty sure that she hadn't given birth there. She must have brought her kit to the house at a later date, but why? Did she know that food might be available here? Perhaps she had come around during the winter, when I put out seeds for the birds. Had she reasoned that settling down near a source of food meant that she didn't have to leave the youngster alone while she went to forage for food?

I opened the window. "Who's a clever girl, then?" I asked. She responded in a low, rumbling voice. I was later to learn that raccoons have quite a large vocabulary, some versions of which they use among themselves, and others in various situations ranging from excitement to danger.

Two days later, I was amazed to see her with five kits! No wonder the poor little creature was hungry if she'd been nursing that lot! The usual litter consists of three to four young, and she was so very tiny. The kits soon reached the stage where they wanted solid food, even though they were not yet weaned. I was kept busy chopping up apples and tearing up pieces of bread for them. Sitting bolt upright with their heads thrown back while they chewed greedily, choking down their meal, they often fell over backwards onto the grass, which was funny to watch.

As the kits grew, Clooney took them elsewhere during the day, but they still arrived in the evening for a meal. It was amusing to see her striding down the path on long legs while they followed in single file, stumbling along in an effort to keep up.

At first, she growled at me when I stepped outside with the food, but she soon learned to trust me with her babies. Each time I opened the door, they would run to me, tapping me on the legs with their little black fingers. I never tried to touch them in return. Raccoons, with their long claws, can be vicious when attacked. Although they were always gentle with me, I treated them with respect. I had no wish to make pets of them. More so than many other wild animals, raccoons are at the mercy of predators, and I didn't want them to lose their sense of self-preservation.

The Paddling Pool

Once again that summer was extremely hot. The lawns dried up and the grass, now straw-like, crackled underfoot. There was little in the way of wild food, such as berries, and bears were coming closer to human habitation in the hope of finding something to eat. Clooney's little crew were all right, with me to provide their meals, but I felt sorry for them as they lolled about in the shade of the lilacs, made languid by the heat.

I wondered why Clooney didn't take the kits to the pond to cool off. It is just a short distance from the house, and raccoons like to swim. I well remember the time I saw an enormous raccoon, surely the granddaddy of them all, swimming on his back in that same pond.

An idea came to me. I would give the kits a paddling pool! Unfortunately, the only suitable container I could find was an unused cat-litter tray, which was really too small for the job. *Oh well,* I thought, *they can drink the water if nothing else.* I took the tray out to the lawn, filled it up, and waited. I was utterly amazed by what happened next.

As soon as I was back inside the house, Clooney stepped into the tub and began to paddle rhythmically in the cold water. Her eyes were closed and she seemed to me to be in a blissful dream. I was delighted with the success of my ploy. The surprising part about this was that, instead of scrambling to get in beside her, the five kits stood in an orderly line, waiting patiently for their turn!

Finally she climbed out and stood back. The first kit stepped into the water and the process was repeated until all five had enjoyed a turn. I did not have a camera handy and I truly wish that somebody else had been with me to witness the scene. It sounds unbelievable, I know, but it did happen. I can't explain how or why this little raccoon made her youngsters wait while she enjoyed herself, but I was reminded of a little episode that was told to me, years ago, concerning a woman I knew. The mother of twelve young children, she was married to a labourer who was frequently out of work. No doubt about it, her life was hard.

One day a neighbour reported that this woman had been seen in the local dairy, sipping a milkshake, while her assorted children waited outside with their noses pressed to the glass. She was criticized severely for this, with more than one well-to-do matron telling her she was an "unnatural mother." But as she remarked to me later, resentful at the interference, "I've got to have something to keep me going." I could certainly see both points of view.

As for Clooney, who knows what was going through her mind, if anything, when she took first turn at the tub? Perhaps it was simply a natural instinct to take what was offered when the chance came along, yet that doesn't explain the well-disciplined behaviour of the kits as they waited in line. I had expected to see an undignified scramble as they jockeyed for position, but that didn't happen.

Whatever the explanation may have been for this behaviour, I'm glad that I was there to see it.

Death of a Mother

Alas, nothing in nature ever stays the same. One day, Clooney arrived with half her tail missing. Perhaps she had been in a fight with another animal, such as a fisher, or a large carnivorous bird, possibly a Great Horned Owl. She looked at me with such a sad and weary look that I felt she must be suffering, but what could I do? I have never seen such a look of despair in an animal's eyes.

The little family went missing for two days, then the kits returned, very nervous and huddling together. I think that Clooney must have died, for I never saw her again. I have read that kits have been known to stay for days beside the body of a dead mother, and I suspect that something similar had happened in this case. Now they were back with me. I had the fanciful thought that when I had last seen Clooney she had known she was dying and had entrusted their care to me. Silly, perhaps, but the fact remained that they needed help, and I was on the spot.

The kits continued to come to me to be fed, but I worried about what would happen to them when winter came. A mother raccoon stays with her young throughout their first winter, but now Clooney was gone. Would they know enough to survive on their own? I didn't want them to die, so I left the door ajar in an old calf pen, thinking that they could use the hayloft if they chose to do so. I climbed the ladder once or twice and was intrigued to see that the old straw had been scooped up into a series of giant nests, so perhaps that's where they were. Raccoons don't hibernate, but they do den up during the worst weather.

In the wild, raccoons eat a variety of foods, including crayfish, grasshoppers, frogs and snakes, small mammals, turtle eggs, apples, and corn. None of these things are available in winter. The little family began to arrive most nights after dark, and I fed them as usual. Although they enjoyed table scraps, our vet recommended giving them dry dog food, and they seemed to relish that.

The following summer, they still came to see me during the light evenings when I was sitting outside. Sometimes they would lie down beside me; at other times they would tap me on the leg with their long fingers, as if wanting my attention. After a while I was able to "learn" their language. Although raccoons can utter blood-curdling screams when roused, these little ones spoke to me in soft, ape-like grunts. When I replied in kind, they listened with their heads on one side, and I could see them grinning. Goodness knows what I was telling them. Whatever it was, they certainly seemed to find it amusing!

When they heard about this, my grown children thought it was all very funny. "Someday they'll produce kits of their own, and then you'll be a raccoon's grandmother," my daughter teased. Nowadays my granddaughter refers to me as "the raccoon whisperer," which is as good a description as any.

Cleo's Kit

Another winter had passed. Clooney's kits were now two years old, and still coming to visit me. They denned up during bad weather, so when there were snowstorms they didn't appear. Then, when the skies cleared, all five would present themselves at my door, quietly lining up and waiting for their evening meal. I was amazed and pleased that they had survived for so long; with so many predators around, the mortality rate for raccoons is high. In July, I noticed that they were arriving from different directions, which indicated that they were now leading independent lives, while still seeming to recognize their kin.

There were three males and two females in this little family, and it was my fond hope that someday Clooney's grandkits would appear. Although I was something of a foster parent to the kits after their mother died, I expected that they would go their separate ways in due course, never to be seen by me again.

As they entered their third year, I experienced a small flicker of hope. None of the wildlife books on my shelf said anything about the age at which raccoons normally have kits. Perhaps they were too young? (I have since heard that it is not unknown for a yearling female to give birth.) And just because their tiny mother, desperate with five kits to feed, had come to me for help, that didn't mean that history would repeat itself.

Clooney had begun hanging around the house in May. She had shown me her first kit on June 16, and had brought out the other four three days later. So during this May, I kept a careful lookout, only to be disappointed. Four raccoons appeared on a regular basis, but the lone female among them did not look to be in an interesting condition.

Then, on June 26, one of the females appeared at eight o'clock in the morning, standing on her hind legs and gazing up at my bedroom window. (I usually threw their food out of this window because in wintertime the snow was too deep for me to struggle around to that side of the house.) This *was* odd. My group made a habit of coming in the early evening. During the next few days, she arrived at regular intervals, and seemed to be taking shelter under the wooden deck. Could it be? This was what Clooney had done two years earlier.

Raccoons are born blind and weighing about two ounces. After their eyes open they begin to move about, and the mother carries them about by the scruff of the neck, much as a cat does with her kittens.

This latest development was interesting. I gave the little female the name of Cleo, and wondered, *did she have kits hidden under the deck?* I got down on my hands and knees and tried to peer underneath, but it was too dark to see anything. I would have to wait and see.

Such disappointment! The end of the month came and nothing had happened.

And then, wonder of wonders, on the evening of July 7, Cleo came to the door accompanied by one very large and robust kit. When I stepped outside, she came to stand beside me, obviously lapping up the praise as I told her what a clever girl she was! Her little black eyes were gleaming with what seemed like pride and satisfaction. The kit looked at me in alarm. Once or twice he sidled up to his mother, chatting to her in a soft voice before retreating to the edge of the deck. The cats were interested, too, studying the newcomer with their noses wrinkling.

I can no longer let my cats wander outside because there are too many dangers here. Fishers prey on cats, as do Great Horned Owls. So we had a long porch built on to the side of the house, enclosed with steel mesh screens from floor to ceiling. This room overlooks the deck and is shaded by a bank of lilacs. Here the cats relax on summer days, birdwatching to their hearts' content. The raccoons often come to take a look inside. I expect that when

I'm out there it's a case of cupboard love, but I do find it amusing when they chatter to the cats from the other side of the screen.

Because Clooney had produced her biggest kit first, bringing the smaller ones out later, I half expected Cleo to do the same, but it seemed that she had only one kit. I've since seen her striding across the lawn, the little one stumbling in her wake. He (or she) is much bigger than Clooney's kits were when I first saw them. Perhaps this is because he was the only one in the litter, or maybe Cleo kept him hidden for a longer period. He wasn't weaned yet, but he did enjoy the chopped apple and bits of bread crust I threw to him.

And so the cycle of life goes on. I feel extraordinarily privileged to have observed these events. Mind you, raccoons are well-known for intruding into the world of humans. They occasionally have to be evicted from people's attics, where they have settled in for the winter. Because of this, friends have warned me not to encourage them, although with thousands or trees on the property there is no shortage of places for them to find the natural dens they are supposed to prefer.

My association with Clooney's kits can only be described as a friendship. It is delightful to sit outside on a summer evening with one or two of them lying down beside me, like little dogs. They are so quiet and gentle — until a strange raccoon tries to butt in! Then the air is rent with blood-curdling screams as they send the intruder on his way. So the saga continues. The knowledge that their life in the wild may not be a lengthy one — Clooney's early death reminds me of that — make such little encounters as these seem all the more precious.

A Nursery Discovered

It had been several years since Clooney first brought her kits to me, and as each successive little raccoon family made its way to me, I wondered where they were being born. *The Audubon Field Guide to North American Mammals* says that the female "prefers to make a leaf nest in large hollow trees, but may also use such protected places as culverts, caves and rock clefts."[1]

One year, in late spring, I was sure that a raccoon had a den in a large tree that had fallen across one of the trails near a small pond. Each time the dogs ran past, I heard warning shrieks and growls which I guessed came from a mother raccoon, protecting her young.

---

1. John D. Whitaker Jr. *The Audubon Society Field Guide to North American Mammals* (New York: Alfred A. Knopf, 1980), 563.

Two of Clooney's kits were female, and no doubt they, in turn, produced young of their own, and would require separate quarters.

The following year, squirrels had chewed their way into a box containing telephone wires on the outside wall of the house, and had built a nest there. Having evicted them, I wanted to find a small piece of tin to cover their entrance hole; I thought there might be some in the old woodshed. Not long after we had moved to Poison Ivy Acres, a fine new shed was built with separate bays for different types of wood. The old building became a repository for window screens, odd bits of lumber, and other bits and pieces that might prove useful in the future.

I stepped inside the door and heard the familiar little chirp with which the raccoons greet me, then I saw that I wasn't alone. A female raccoon had appropriated a large cardboard box, perhaps three feet square, and had carefully lined it with chopped-up newspaper. This, I supposed, was her nursery. From where I was standing, I couldn't tell whether she had already given birth or was preparing to do so, and I wasn't about to risk taking a closer look.

"Sorry!" I muttered, backing away.

As I closed the door, I could see two fairly large raccoons huddled together under a plank at the back of the shed. I'm guessing that these constituted the female's litter from the year before.

Again, the Audubon book suggests that some young raccoons disperse in the autumn, while others remain, only to be driven away before the mother bears the next litter, so I don't know how this applies to what I saw. I do know that raccoons who bring their kits to me in May usually keep the youngsters with them all during the following winter, with the occasional absence of a few days in bad weather. This means that I'm usually feeding seven or eight every night!

There was one very bad winter, though, when no fewer than thirteen raccoons showed up. I was hard put to find enough scraps for each one to have a mouthful or two. They all accepted what there was, without squabbling. *Where had they all come from?* I wondered. *And how did they know enough to arrive together at a time when I'd be looking out for them?* It looked like a family reunion of sorts! Or do animals have some secret method of passing the word around to others like themselves?

The following summer there was a tragic occurrence quite close to home. I knew that some of the raccoons had been sheltering inside the sugar shack, going in underneath the main door where the gravel is worn down. One morning, I was cutting grass on the lawn nearby, and everything seemed to be quiet and peaceful. But, being badly stung by Deer Flies, I went back to the house for protective clothing. When I returned half an hour later, I was saddened to find some raccoon remains on the ground outside the shack. Piecing the story together, I surmised that a fisher had chased the raccoon back to the shack, catching it by the tail as it tried to get inside, then dragging it out for the kill. It must have been lurking nearby all the time I was busily mowing.

A DESPERATE BATTLE

According to some wildlife books, a raccoon, when being hunted down, will lure a dog to water. "A dog that swims well can easily overtake a raccoon in the water, but the raccoon, a furious fighter, can then whip a single dog."[2]

This may sound like a tall tale, but I know it is true, for I have seen it happen. Our Gordon Setter, Rusty, was a strong dog, much more so than either of our gentle English Setters or Bunny, our Irish Setter. Rusty was a year old before he came to us, and pretty set in his ways. He was a strong swimmer, well-trained in the art of sitting quietly in a canoe, and he loved to ride with us in the car. He was affectionate with the family, gentle with the cats, and thoroughly trustworthy with Laura, my baby granddaughter.

His one failing was that he was territorial and could be aggressive with strangers, either man or beast, who invaded his space — especially if he thought I was being threatened. Picking up the mail one day at the country store, I inadvertently left a package on the counter. I was about to drive off when another customer, who knew me, dashed after me to return it. Being closest to the passenger side of the car he tried to open that door. Fortunately it was locked. Rusty, who wasn't wearing his seat belt since we were not far from home, flew to the front of the car in a rage. I dread to think what might have happened if the poor man had managed to open that door. Strangely, I knew that if I had taken the dog into the store anyone could have patted him, and he'd have lapped up the attention, rolling onto his back and waving his legs in the air.

The following episode happened a few years before Clooney came on the scene, and it came close to being Rusty's undoing. I have never seen a raccoon as big as the one he tangled with one autumn morning. The size did not deter the dog. Yelping madly, he set off in pursuit. The raccoon plunged into the pond and began swimming on its back with one

---

2. John D. Whitaker Jr. *The Audubon Society Field Guide to North American Mammals* (New York: Alfred A. Knopf, 1980), 563.

paw held high in the air, vicious claws extended. Rusty dived into the water, and the raccoon prepared to fight to the death. It snatched at one of Rusty's front legs and dived under the water, taking the dog with it.

Moments later, the pair came to the surface again, but Rusty's blood was up. Once more, they disappeared beneath the water. I was desperate. Surely this was one battle that the dog couldn't win. I slid down the bank into the water, hoping to get hold of the dog's collar. Admittedly, it was a foolish thing to do, but what choice did I have? This was a well-loved dog and it would have broken my heart if he had died in that manner.

The combatants came to the surface and went down for the third time. I doubt they even knew I was there, but luckily Rusty decided to call it a day. He swam to the bank and climbed out, shaking himself violently. His paw was badly mauled, and he had to be taken to the vet for stitches. It was his own fault, of course, and no one could blame his adversary. Did Rusty learn a lesson from this encounter, you may ask? The answer is no. Porcupines, skunks, and groundhogs remained on his list for annihilation, although he behaved perfectly well around cattle, sheep, and horses. Who can tell what goes on in the mind of a dog? Rusty was certainly an enigma.

 RUFUS

My dear cat Ginger died at the age of eighteen, when a fine September was just beginning. To be more exact, he had to be euthanized. His systems were beginning to shut down, and it would have been cruel to condemn him to a lingering death. Sweet-natured to the last, he sat on my lap, purring, as we awaited our turn to see the vet.

There were four cats still at home. Smokey, Ginger's litter mate, would live to be almost twenty-two years of age. Blackie Ryan was now at the head of the pecking order, with Clancy as his small, devoted sidekick. Ruby, a beautiful red tabby, was the youngest of the gang. All were rescued cats.

How is it that stray cats always seem to know when a vacancy has occurred in a loving home? I have seen this happen again and again, and there is certainly no arguing with the fact that Rufus turned up two weeks after Ginger's death, begging to be taken in.

Coming home one evening, I drove down to the back door and saw a very handsome young cat in the headlights. He was gulping down some leftover pineapple rice that I'd put out for the raccoons. I've reminded him of this many times since, especially when he turns up his nose at some choice morsel offered to him in his little red dish.

Rufus ran off when I got out of the car, but the next evening, he appeared at the kitchen window, watching me feed the other four cats and uttering pitiful cries. This was too much for my soft heart, and I put out a bowl of food on the doorstep. After licking the dish clean, he sauntered off up the lane.

Then the weather turned wet and cold. I propped the porch door open and left a box inside, lined with a piece of old blanket. Each evening, the cat showed up wet and shivering, ate his supper, and put himself to bed. In the morning he strolled up the lane and was gone all day. I hoped that I wasn't luring away some neighbour's beloved pet, but that didn't seem probable, since he had adopted me. Given the date of his arrival, it seemed likely that he was a refugee from the nearby lake. Sometimes uncaring people acquire a cat or dog to take to the cottage as summer companions, only to abandon them when they leave for home on Labour Day.

November came, bringing the snow with it. The porch door couldn't be left open much longer, and the cat needed warmer quarters. Somewhat reluctantly, I decided to add Rufus to my brood. By now all of them were indoor cats, because the world outside was too dangerous for them.

A trip to the veterinarian was in order. Rufus was vaccinated, and given an appointment to return later to be neutered. The vet assessed him as being about eight months old. I mentioned my fears of having taken in someone else's pet. "If they can't give him food and shelter, they don't deserve him," he replied. "In any case, he could be a feral cat," our vet added, trying to reassure me.

I don't think that this was the case, because Rufus was thoroughly socialized. When we reached home, he marched inside, took a tour of the house to learn where the litter boxes, water bowl, and dry-food dishes were located, and then installed himself in a comfortable armchair and went to sleep. The other cats and dogs watched in amazement. When he woke up, he came face to face with Blackie Ryan, who stared him down unblinkingly. Abashed, Rufus backed away, and then proceeded to spray the walls in an attempt to establish his territory.

"Any more of that, my lad, and you'll be back on the road," I told him, as I got out my cleaning supplies. He stared back at me out of big green eyes. I have never met another cat with such a "butter won't melt in my mouth" expression. In time, I learned that this innocent look was deceptive.

For the moment, he was a fine addition to the household. Although very affectionate with people, he was nervous at first when anyone came to the house, hiding behind the fridge until he understood that they were welcome visitors. Then he would rub against their legs, holding his bushy tail high. He was well-tolerated by the other pets and behaved himself beautifully in return. All that changed when Blackie Ryan passed away from diabetes; Rufus suffered an abrupt personality change. The only male cat remaining in the household, he quickly asserted himself as top cat.

Now nine years old, he is as sweet as ever with people, but he can be vicious with other animals. Adjustments have had to be made in the household to cope with this, but that is another story.

 ## A LIFE SAVED

My feelings towards mice are ambivalent. While I'm interested in observing their lives outdoors, I certainly don't appreciate it when they come into the house. My cats are good mousers who are quick to dispatch any small intruder, which leaves me with the problem of disposing of a mangled corpse. Not my favourite job!

I suppose that, in general, I regard mice as valuable members in the food chain. They provide meals for hawks, owls, foxes, and the like, as is nature's intention. However, there was one occasion when I saved the life of a small rodent, and I don't care who knows it. I had come round the corner of the house, to a place where two wings meet, forming an L-shape. The cat was crouched down there with his tail lashing, obviously getting ready to spring.

He had cornered a small Field Mouse, which was obviously aware that it hadn't long to live. However, this was nothing like the "cow'rin tim'rous beastie" known to the poet Robert Burns. This little creature was up on its hind legs, waving its front paws aggressively like a trainee boxer, willing to engage this Goliath of a cat in mortal combat. Of course it didn't have a hope of coming out the winner, and any attempt to dash past the cat would have resulted in instant death. Still, I could only admire the tiny rodent's bravado. Faced with impossible odds, it was prepared to go down fighting.

Visions of the way in which the British people behaved after the defeat at Dunkirk raced through my head. Dozens of small craft had crossed the English Channel to bring home the thousands of men who were stranded on the beaches, within range of the enemy guns. I had grown up hearing so many stories about this saga of gallantry that for years I believed it had been a victory for the Allies, and in a way, I suppose, it was. The mouse, too, seemed to embody an indomitable spirit, and I was determined that it should live to fight another day. I snatched up the cat and carried him into the house, while he grumbled and fought me every step of the way.

Perhaps I was behaving like an idiot, but I've always had sympathy for the underdog, and this mouse certainly fit the profile. I wanted it to have a second chance. To this day, I have a clear memory of that sparring mouse. This story does illustrate how strong the instinct for survival can be, whether in man or in beast.

Just to set the record straight, I must mention that I've been waging war on the mice that find their way into my detached garage. I had purchased a new car in October, and I was looking forward to having a trouble-free winter with it. You can imagine my shock when I received an email from On*Star customer service, advising me that the vehicle should be checked out immediately because they suspected trouble with the braking system, the steering, the transmission, and much more.

Cursing all modern computerized vehicles, I returned the car to the dealership, where the puzzled technicians had to put in several hours of exploration before they discovered the source of the problem. A mouse had chewed its way through a wire! The problem was easily put right, but I was faced with a large bill because of the hours of labour involved.

Now the mice are treated to delicious bacon-flavoured tidbits, which will dispatch them in short order — I hope!

A DREAM OF MOOSE

Sometimes, in the depths of a harsh winter, when life at Poison Ivy Acres is reduced to a matter of sheer survival, I'm seized with a longing for something unusual to happen. Sometimes this wish comes true. An uncommon bird may arrive at the feeder, blown off course by a fierce windstorm. Or a variety of tracks in the snow may bear witness to some interaction between the species. One December morning, I discovered that a whole flock of Wild Turkeys had been to my door, looking for something to eat, I daresay, and they had then marched up the lane en route to the hayfields where they spend much of their time.

Alas, the daily ration of sunflower seeds had been consumed by the smaller visitors to the bird feeders and there was nothing left over for the turkeys. Their trip had been in vain.

For years now, I've been hoping to see a moose here. This is not as ridiculous as it may seem. In our corner of Ontario, we are just a few miles from the province of Quebec, the border being the mighty Ottawa River. Moose abound across the river in Pontiac County, which is referred to locally as "the Pontiac." Occasionally, in winter, a moose will wander across the river and turn up in some unexpected place, such as the outskirts of Ottawa or places farther north. In fact, a few years ago one was seen just outside the town of Renfrew, where I do my shopping.

Moose also inhabit Algonquin Provincial Park, which is not far from the northern edge of Renfrew County. The Moose (*Alces alces*) belongs to the Family *Cervidae*, Order *Artiodactyla*. *Moose* is an Aboriginal word for this large animal. The Latin *alce* translates as *elk*, which is the name given to this species by Europeans. In Canada, however, the name *elk* refers to a different species, so the name *moose* is used for the animal found here.

This is the young moose who was tangled up in the reeds. It was rescued and returned safely to its anxious mother.

So far, no moose has come to Poison Ivy Acres, but hope springs eternal. DW's photo of a moose calf hangs in my kitchen, where it is much admired by visitors. It is a close-up shot. Most people think it must have been taken with a telephoto lens, but this was not the case.

DW and his friend, Earl, were staying at a club they belonged to in the Pontiac when they came upon a cow moose, bellowing frantically at the edge of a lake. The cause of her distress was easy to see: a very young calf was caught in the reeds at some distance from the shore, and she seemed powerless to help it. Moose are excellent swimmers, and their young usually acquire this skill by the age of about six weeks. This youngster, however, was unable to manage on its own.

The two men were in a dilemma. The calf couldn't be left to die a lingering death, yet to interfere could mean trouble. The full-grown moose is as big as a horse. A bull moose can weigh from nine hundred to fourteen hundred pounds; a cow seven hundred to one thousand pounds. As anyone knows, it is unwise to accost a wild animal with its young,

Mother and baby reunited. Strangely, the cow seemed to sense that the intruders meant no harm to her calf, and she watched from a safe distance, not missing a movement.

and moose can be unpredictable and dangerous. Under normal circumstances they avoid human contact, but cows with calves are fiercely protective.

DW took a number of photos of the stranded animal. Then, taking a deep breath, Earl waded into the water, picked up the calf, and brought it safely to the bank. All the while the cow stood quietly watching, as if she knew that the men meant well by her baby. As they walked away, the pair looked back to see the calf reunited with its mother. It was an experience they were never to forget.

I have seen moose from the air, but have never met one face to face. Until that day comes, I have the photo on my kitchen wall to remind me that the natural world is full of surprises.

MIDNIGHT STANDOFF

It was the night of the full moon. Loath to turn in, I stood at the bedroom window taking in the scene. It was almost as bright as day, and I was hoping to see or hear an owl, as it went about its nightly business.

A dark shape was silently waddling across the lawn, heading my way. It was an enormous porcupine, and I knew from experience that it would cross the deck on its way to the woods on the north side of the house, possibly making for the creek. In the shadow of the lilacs, another creature waited, unseen by both of us, until it emerged to face the intruder. Then I saw the white stripes on its black fur. A skunk!

I wondered which of them would give way. For a few moments they seemed to be facing each other down. Then the skunk turned its back, but that was not a sign of retreat. A characteristic odour filled the air. The porcupine must have got the stinging fluid right in the face. Whether it had time to retaliate I couldn't tell, but I wouldn't mind betting that the skunk received a snout full of quills. Practising shallow breathing, I closed the window, and saw no more.

Much like people, wild things are creatures of routine. In some cases this is easily explained; birds return to my feeders day after day because they expect to find food there. Birds who are summer visitors to Poison Ivy Acres return in spring to the nesting site they occupied the year before. Animals, too, have their regular habits. Each year a female raccoon transfers her kits from their birthplace to the dark retreat underneath my deck, where they remain in safety until their eyes are open at the age of about three weeks. This shows some careful thinking on the part of the mother, who knows she is close to a food source that will sustain her until the kits are weaned.

Other animals, particularly nocturnal ones, seem to move about for no apparent reason, yet using a prescribed path. There are four lawns here; one is near the deck, with the pond and some mixed bush on the far side. When it's almost time to mow this expanse of grass, it's obvious from the narrow, well-trodden path in the middle that animals have crossed from the bush and gone past the house on their way to some unknown destination. Why they have done this on a regular basis, and what their purpose might be, is a matter for some speculation.

A porcupine is a frequent user of this secret trail. I have occasionally woken up on a summer night, alerted by the sound of its claws clicking on the wood as it crosses the deck. This calls for immediate action because porcupines destroy wood, and I live in a log house!

Porcupines love to chew on wood, so Poison Ivy Acres, with all its log buildings, is paradise for them. Here, one inspects the woodshed.

In winter, there is always at least one porcupine at work beside the lane, stripping the bark from the sumacs and other softwood trees. There are thousands of trees on Poison Ivy Acres, and I can spare a few. I don't even mind when a porcupine invades the open woodshed to attack a log there. But I draw the line at letting it chomp on a corner of the house. Staying at a safe distance, I have to go outside and bang two metal pots together to try to drive it away.

Skunks come closer to the house in the fall. They head for one of the south-facing lawns, where they spend the night digging for grubs. In the morning, I'll find little divots of earth lying around all over the place where the skunk has been working. Although skunks don't hibernate, they do fatten themselves up in the fall, as a way to compensate for the winter months when there is little food to be found.

I suppose that I'm creature of habit, too. Before turning in for the night, I always glance out of the window to see what might be going on outside. I don't want to miss anything!

 # GOODBYE TO MY BICYCLE

There was a bicycle at Poison Ivy Acres once. That is, the bicycle is still here, but it is lacking many of its component parts. It used to be a smart, shiny green machine, but today it is only a shadow of its former self.

At one time, I had to pick up my mail at a group box three miles from home, which meant a healthy six-mile trip to receive it. Sometimes I walked, but more often I cycled, trudging up the steep hills and whizzing down on the other side.

I loved that bicycle. Sadly, so did my neighbourhood porcupine. He, or she, was so enormous that I wondered if it was a pregnant female. I made sure that nothing was left lying about outside that was likely to attract its attention, but I didn't think about my poor bicycle, standing in the lean-to beside the garage.

I went out one morning to discover that something had enjoyed a feast in the night, and "porky" was the obvious suspect. The bike was lying on its side, but I hadn't heard the crash it must have made as it fell, because the garage is on the far side of the yard. Tires, saddle, and cable brakes had all been chewed. Even the hard rubber on the pedals bore teeth marks. The soft rubber covering the handlebars had provided a tasty dessert. Standing there, fuming, I could only hope that the porcupine was now suffering from indigestion. I was reminded of the time when a painted boat, stored in the open drive shed, had received similar treatment.

Why do porcupines do this? People have offered various suggestions, but none seem sensible to me. My property abounds in trees and clover, free for the taking, but that doesn't seem to be enough for these vegetarian animals. It is a known fact that they like salt. *The Audubon Society Field Guide to North American Mammals* offers the interesting fact that the animal "has a great appetite for wooden tool handles that have absorbed human perspiration through use."[3]

I suppose this is as good an explanation as any for what happened to my bicycle. I certainly managed to lose a lot of moisture when toiling uphill, although how that affected my pedals and brakes I can't say! One can only suppose that after chewing the interesting bits, the porcupine was having too good a time to give up. One thing is certain, the world of wildlife is filled with mystery.

A friend suggests that leaving out a bowl of salt will help; the theory being that the porcupine will go for that and leave the woodwork alone. I'm afraid that if I do that, though, the word will spread and the hordes will be upon us.

I once had a narrow escape. In the midst of gardening, I dashed into the open woodshed to fetch a hoe. Instead of hanging it up after the last time I'd used it I had left it propped up against a log pile. Without looking where I was going I reached in to retrieve it. Suddenly, I became aware of a pair of bright eyes watching me, and saw to my dismay that I had come within inches of touching a porcupine. Luckily for me the animal had its back to the woodpile, otherwise it would have meant a quick trip to the emergency room.

While it is a myth that porcupines can shoot their quills, as many people still believe, they can inflict a great deal of damage simply by lashing their tails in the direction of an enemy. I could almost feel the pain!

---

3. John D. Whitaker Jr. *The Audubon Society Field Guide to North American Mammals* (New York: Alfred A. Knopf, 1980), 529.

PLAYING DEAD

It's well-known that some animals, faced with imminent death and no way of retreat, will try to evade capture by pretending to be dead. Scientists suggest that some predators that prefer to kill their prey before eating it will ignore anything they believe to be already dead. Obviously, playing dead won't help when the captor is something like an owl, which flies away with its catch when it is still alive, but in other cases it has been known to work.

I have encountered this behaviour twice. The first time was in the case of the newborn fawn I have already described; the second time it occurred inside the house. As so often happens, I learned more about this phenomenon from my domestic animals.

I was upstairs in my office when I heard sounds of a scuffle coming from the kitchen below. When I went down to investigate, I found Rufus standing in front of the fridge, his tail lashing furiously. Three of the other cats were in various places downstairs, minding their own business, but little Clancy was nowhere to be seen. I called and called, but she failed to appear.

Rufus pawed at the floor, like a miniature bull, then sprang up onto the dryer and peered behind the fridge. I wasn't sure what was going on, but if he had a mouse back there I didn't want it to be killed in a spot I couldn't reach. Shutting him in another room I hopped up on the dryer and tried to see what was behind it.

There are water tanks behind the wall, which can be reached only by pulling out the fridge. To one side of the tanks, the pipes go down through a depression filled with gravel. Clancy was lying on her side in there, not moving. Rufus had already attacked her once or twice before, biting her on the neck as she struggled to escape, and I was convinced that he had killed her now. There was no response when I whispered her name.

I tried to move the heavy fridge, something I had never managed to do before. Desperation lent me strength, and I managed to pull it forward to the point where I was able to squeeze behind it. Smokey and Blackie Ryan, both looking alarmed, came to see what was happening. I couldn't get close enough to lift Clancy out. She still didn't respond, and she didn't seem to be breathing. I was sure that she was dead.

I put some of her favourite treats on the floor behind the fridge. After a while she stirred, sniffing the air, and then climbed out of the hole and came to eat the tasty morsels. I was able to reach her then and out we both came, much to my relief.

Nowadays my cats often rush to hide behind the fridge, especially when they see me coming with their carrying cases, which signal a trip to the vet! In such cases they remain on their feet, ready to flee again if necessary. In Clancy's case it was different. I know that she was truly "playing dead" in order to baffle her tormentor. Until that moment, I hadn't realized that domestic pets can use this technique. I had thought it was adopted only by creatures in the wild.

As for Rufus, his behaviour towards Clancy became worse after Blackie Ryan died. No matter what I tried, he continued to bother her and was particularly aggressive when she was using the litter box. I didn't want to give him away, but Clancy had to be protected. Luckily this is a big house. The problem was solved by having her live upstairs and letting Rufus have the run of the downstairs rooms. Because I spend so much time in my upstairs office, Clancy is never lonely. It may not be the ideal solution, but it works.

PART II:
OF LAND AND SKY

A BEAUTIFUL SIGHT

When I think back over the years, I realize that I have seen many beautiful things at Poison Ivy Acres. Among the bird visitors, I relish an occasional sighting of Scarlet Tanagers with their vivid plumage, or the handsome Rose-breasted Grosbeaks that come here in the spring.

Many colourful wildflowers grow here. These include the moccasin-shaped Yellow Lady's Slippers in the hardwood bush, and I have often found Fringed Gentians at the edge of the creek and Dutchman's Breeches beside the line fence. Red Columbines and Dame's Rocket grow closer to the house, and violets of various colours grow here and there. The most welcome are the tiny Hepaticas that grow beside the lane, because their appearance signals the end of winter and the return of spring.

Colourful fungi, such as the *Amanita muscaria* and the various Coral Mushrooms, are always a delight to the eye, springing up in the cedar bush after a spell of wet weather. And while I would be hard pressed to suggest a favourite among these things, I have to say that I cherish the memory of something quite different that I only saw once, and never again.

There was a mist across the land that morning, as I set out for a walk with the dogs, forecasting a hot day to come. This was a fairly short walk, a circuit taking us down through the beaver meadow, because I had many things to do that day. The dogs bounded ahead, happily investigating the various scents, with Rusty searching for some beaver scat to roll in but, luckily for me, not finding any.

Then I saw something that made me catch my breath in awe. There are many dead trees in the beaver flood where the beaver dams have widened the creek. On that morning it seemed that every one of them was festooned with a large, lacy spider's web, trembling with drops of moisture. The sun, peeping through the mist, made these shine like silver. No decorated Christmas tree could come close to the glory of this phenomenon. A veritable army of spiders must have been at work there throughout the night.

I desperately wanted a record of this unusual sight. As fast as I could, I ran the quarter mile back to the house to fetch a camera; but, alas, when I returned, this fleeting vision of nature's work was gone. I suppose that the webs were still there, but they were no long visible from the bank. It was a sad disappointment. So many times since then I have gone down to the beaver meadow early in the morning in the hope that the spiders have been at work, but nothing remotely like it has been seen since, even though others have also looked for it.

The dogs were happy, of course, having benefited from a double run that morning, so it's an ill wind that blows nobody any good, as the old people used to say.

 ## THE SOUND OF SILENCE

Visitors from the city invariably comment on the quiet here. "It's so peaceful," they murmur, as they look around. And I suppose it does seem quiet to them, compared with the sounds of traffic and the comings and goings of numerous people going about their daily round. It's been more than twenty years since I last visited the city, and even then I found it to be a shock to the senses. When I reached home after my last trip there, my ears were still ringing from the noise of the pneumatic drills used in downtown construction. I asked myself if I really wanted to go there again, short of some sort of emergency. All my life, when visiting cities, I'd always headed for their parks and green spaces rather than the fine restaurants and glitzy shopping malls, which should have told me something.

Peaceful it may be at Poison Ivy Acres, but it's hardly silent. For those who have ears to hear, the air is filled with sound and music. In the spring, birds advertise for mates at all hours of the day, whether they be chickadees with their whistling mating call or Great-crested Flycatchers with their distinctive "wheep."

At night in late winter, owls hoot repeatedly. In the spring, Whip-poor-wills repeat the call that gives them their name. While it is good to hear these birds, which, sadly, are becoming less common in our area, their calls can drive a person mad. I remember having to get up to close the bedroom window after hearing a Whip-poor-will sending his message from the nearby spruce tree no fewer than twenty-eight times. My closing the window frightened him away and he flew off to a tree on the other side of the lawn, which gave me some relief.

Then there are woodpeckers who, in addition to drilling for food, seemingly drum with their beaks to get attention from the opposite sex. When this happens on a steel roof, it conjures up unhappy memories of visits to the dentist back in the days when local anesthetics were seldom used. Other spring sounds involve the drumming of the partridge, and the winnowing sound of the snipe, coming back to earth after a dazzling display of aerial manoeuvres.

In summer, when the birds have paired off and are engaged in rearing their young, the air is filled with the sounds peculiar to each species. Robins, Catbirds, Phoebes, and Blue

Jays all add their voices to the mix. The tiny wren has a staccato voice out of all proportion to its size: it stutters like a tiny machine gun.

Animals, too, give voice from time to time. When I have inadvertently come up unseen behind a White-tailed Deer I've been treated to a surprised huff before the creature bounds off. When my local raccoons feel like holding a conversation with me, we exchange soft grunts. My cat Ruby wails furiously when a stray cat wanders by; if it dares to linger, her voice rises to a crescendo as she vents her rage.

Weather, too, provides its own sounds. It is good to lie in bed when the wind howls outside, and rain patters on the roof. When there is a west wind, trees may come down in the night, but that won't become apparent until morning.

Thunderstorms are unpleasant, and, when my well was struck by lightning, the noise was so loud that I felt my heart jump in my chest. The animals know when a storm is coming long before I do, and whenever I see Clancy disappearing under the bed, I know that it's time to take action in case the power goes off. Containers have to be filled with drinking water, and a flashlight must be located. In the morning the sound of the waterfall is heard, as rainwater runs through the culvert and splashes down to the pond below.

Yes, it is peaceful here at Poison Ivy Acres, but silent it is not, no matter what my city visitors may think. Perhaps their hearing has been blunted by the daily cacophony of sound that is their diet in their urban surroundings.

SOME ADVENTURES WITH TURTLES

I think that turtles are fascinating creatures, and every summer I seem to learn a little more about them. Canada has ten species of inland turtles, and representatives of three of these share Poison Ivy Acres with us.

We have a saying in the country: "If you want to see a bear, go where a bear is." The same can be said of turtles. This is the perfect place for them, complete with a creek and several ponds.

Each summer they emerge from the marshes and head for the lane. This half-mile expanse of gravel road, plus a short branch that bypasses my kitchen window, is a favourite nesting site for dozens of turtles. The familiar Eastern Painted Turtle (*Chrysemys picta picta*), the less common Blanding's (*Emydoidea blandingii*), and the fearsome snapper (*Chelydra*

A turtle lays her eggs, using a hind foot to dig a hole, and later to cover up the nesting site. Unfortunately, many of the eggs are soon found and dug up by raccoons or skunks.

serpentina serpentina) all choose to lay their eggs here. The female digs a hole, deposits her eggs, covers the site, and departs. When the eggs hatch, the young turtles are on their own from day one.

Unfortunately many of the sites, particularly the shallow holes dug by Painted Turtles, are soon robbed by raccoons and skunks, which leave the broken, oval shells lying on the ground. Still, many do survive, because the painted turtle is quite common here.

Turtles are equipped with an egg tooth, which enables them to slash their way out of the egg. This tooth is shed when the turtle is a few weeks old. After hatching, the newborns work their way up to the surface to greet the world. On one occasion, we were lucky enough to observe a clutch of tiny turtles emerging from the sandbank beside the pond, where their lives had begun.

Years ago I did a foolish thing. I was mowing the lawn when, out of the corner of my eye, I noticed a slight movement in the grass. On investigation I found a small painted turtle whose carapace was about one-and-a-half inches long. Some instinct takes the young creatures from their birthplace to the marsh or pond, but my little turtle seemed to be lacking this basic knowledge. It was covered in dust and it didn't retreat into its shell as older turtles do. I realize now that it must have just emerged into the light and was probably disoriented. Left to itself, it would probably have found its way in time. My only excuse for intervening is that it was too dangerous to leave it in the path of the lawn mower or in the way of anyone who might drive in.

Deciding to give it a helping hand, I carried it down to the pond, about three hundred yards away, and placed it in the grass at the edge. It immediately scuttled into the water and, swimming bravely, struck out for the opposite shore. After a while its little legs began to falter, and it began to sink. The pond is ten feet deep at that point and a guilty feeling came over me. *Had I lured the unsuspecting young turtle to its doom?*

Feeling rather foolish, I launched the raft and paddled to the middle of the pond, where the young turtle was rapidly losing strength. I leaned over and scooped it up and returned it to the water's edge, where it disappeared into the rushes. I resolved to observe the golden rule from then on. Take note! It is usually best to leave nature alone. We live, and learn. And when we learn, wild things may live.

Since that time I have taken part in several herpetofaunal surveys, where it has been my duty to record the species and numbers of turtles, snakes, frogs, and toads at Poison Ivy Acres. The dogs and cats are great helpers in this work. They're always eager to point out turtles, which seem to fascinate them.

When I find painted turtles, the ones laying eggs usually have a carapace of about six inches in length. Painted turtles love to bask in the sun, and on bright days it is possible to see several dozen or so much larger ones sunning themselves on a floating log in a slough. Some of these have a carapace of more than a foot long. I like to think of them as superannuated turtles, enjoying retirement from the reproductive life. (Unless, of course, they are males having a bonding session while the females are away laying their eggs!)

I find the Blanding's Turtles even more intriguing. Although similar in size to the painted turtles, they have a humped carapace. We have learned that when you pick up one of these timid creatures, it is wise to hold it well away from you as it will invariably be startled into releasing a very large amount of water. I marvel that one small creature can hold so much!

The female Blanding's can often be seen here on July evenings while searching for a nesting site. The eggs of these turtles are round, like miniature golf balls. On one occasion,

*Having notified
his owners that a
Snapping Turtle
is lurking nearby,
Charlie retreats to a
safe distance. Both
dogs and cats alike are
thrilled by the arrival
of these slow-moving
creatures.*

104

the chosen spot was right outside my kitchen door, where there was little chance of the eggs hatching because the car is often parked there. Added to that, on hot days the dogs excavate cool places on the same spot for themselves to lie in. With this in mind, and curious to see how many eggs there might be, I carefully uncovered the cavity, finding the eggs about four inches below the surface There were fourteen. I covered them up again, but, as I suspected, they never did hatch out.

Perhaps the most misunderstood turtle of all is the Snapping Turtle. It can weigh as much as fifty pounds and it has powerful jaws, which are necessary for its own protection because it is unable to withdraw completely into its shell. If attacked or teased, it is capable of inflicting a serious wound. However, it can be handled if one takes care. Like most creatures, it will mind its own business if it doesn't feel threatened. One summer, when a big snapper took up residence in the pond near the house, DW swam there on a regular basis and came to no harm. The turtle simply retreated under the dock until the coast was clear, eager to avoid a confrontation.

Snapping Turtles are fairly common, but one day the species could face extinction because of its treatment by humans. We have heard horror stories of cottagers killing snappers "in case they hurt the children," when any number of more important lessons could be taught to the youngsters after such a sighting.

One summer, DW found fourteen Snapping Turtles crushed to death on a logging road, where they had gone to lay their eggs. Judging by the skid marks on the road, a logger had gone out of his way to kill them. I often wonder what prompts people to make a point of killing defenceless creatures. Perhaps that thoughtless man was a product of a home environment where turtles were not respected.

We had an interesting experience with a big old snapper that inhabited our pond. She arrived outside the kitchen window to dig a nesting cavity. The process took more than an hour as she laboriously scooped up gravel with a hind leg. Another long period elapsed while she attempted to lay eggs in the hole. Nothing happened. Finally she replaced the gravel. The whole process took more than four hours, and all her work had been for nothing. We wondered if this was a very old turtle, incapable of reproducing, yet still possessing the instinct to perform the annual ritual of life.

For me, observing turtles as they go about their daily round is one of the joys of spring and early summer.

The year 2010 was remarkable in that for the first time I saw a turtle run! Because the warm weather came early, the turtles came out to lay their eggs in May instead of June, as they usually did. Setting out for town one morning, I found my way barred by a good-sized Snapping Turtle that was excavating a nesting site in the middle of the lane. Getting out of the car, to make sure there was enough room to pass without causing harm, I approached the turtle, which was one I hadn't seen before. She raised her head and leaned towards me, perhaps preparing to defend herself. Satisfied, I drove away.

When I returned two hours later, I saw that she had dug three holes, apparently rejecting each one as too shallow for her purpose. At that point, there is a shelf of rock under the lane, which had defeated her. The shelf, a relic of the Ice Age, goes far beyond where she was working. Now she was making a fourth attempt, doomed to disappointment because a steel culvert lay below. I couldn't drive on so I gently beeped the horn, hoping she would get the message.

I was amazed when she suddenly stood up, revealing long legs, hoisting her carapace some two feet above the ground. She scuttled off the road and disappeared into the long grass. I had expected to remain seated for some time while she slowly shuffled away, but she was gone in the blink of an eye. The expression "wonders never cease" may be a cliché, but in the world of nature it is apt indeed.

 ## A CAPTIVE BUTTERFLY

I went into the sugar shack one spring day in search of a hatchet, and there I found a beautiful butterfly, beating its wings on the glass as it tried to escape through the window. I forget now what it was; I only recall that it was fairly large as butterflies go, and that it had plenty of colour in it. Possibly it was a Fritillary or a Tortoiseshell.

My heart went out to the poor little thing. The large double doors of the shack were now open wide, and the butterfly could have flown free quite easily, but it kept fluttering at the glass. Gently, I managed to scoop it up in my cupped hands and carry it outside.

The butterfly soared into the air, the very epitome of joy, and then it came down and settled on my head for a moment. That done, it flew away and was never seen again. I am not so foolish as to imagine that the little thing could have been grateful to me for my help, but I do believe that it felt glad to be released from its struggles. I'm sure it would have beaten itself to death if I had not come along at the right time.

The first butterflies come to Poison Ivy Acres even while the snow is still on the ground. Mourning Cloaks, Fritillaries, and the Common Blue are the first to appear. Sometimes we have another snowfall after their arrival, and then I feel sure that these beautiful, fragile things will perish, yet there are always more to be seen in the days that follow.

In due course we see White Admirals, Sulphurs, Buckeyes, Coppers, and Skippers, to name a few. In their infinite variety, butterflies are surely one of nature's great gifts to us, and it is always a joy when one of them stops to rest on my sleeve while I'm out walking.

A little later, when the lilacs are in bloom, they are often covered with Eastern Tiger Swallowtails, with their yellow, brown, and blue markings. During the wet summer of 2009, the swallowtails were late arriving, and by then the lilac blossoms were dead. I wondered what else they could feed on. Referring to my Audubon field guide, I was glad to discover that they can obtain nectar from a wide range of other flowers.

In the autumn, I'm always glad to see the brilliant orange Monarch Butterflies, and I have to marvel that these fragile beauties are able to migrate thousands of miles to the southern United States. Whenever I spot one of them, I look closely to see if it has the extra line that identifies it as a look-alike Viceroy. Nature has developed this resemblance as a defence mechanism for the Viceroy. The larvae of the Monarch feed on milkweed and dogbane plants, giving the butterfly a bitter taste, which renders it unacceptable to predators. Both milkweed and dogbane grow at Poison Ivy Acres.

On summer nights, I sometimes switch on an outside light to see which moths I can attract. My favourite is the Big Poplar Sphinx Moth, which is a very pretty thing. The larvae feed on poplars and willows, both of which are found here in abundance.

The most magnificent moth I have ever seen actually came to my bedroom window, where it perched on the screen for quite some time, enabling me to examine it closely. This was a Luna Moth (*Actias luna*), which is a pale green in colour with a long tail on each hind wing. I have never seen one since, so I know that I was lucky indeed to have had that experience when I did.

LITTLE CRITTERS

When I was quite young, I found myself in hot water with two women who were leaning over a pram, going into raptures over the infant lying inside.

"Do come and look," one of them called to me, and when I obediently came closer I saw a particularly homely specimen of babyhood, blowing bubbles and waving its fists in the air.

'There, don't you think he's absolutely beautiful?" the first woman gushed. I stared gloomily into the baby carriage before uttering the immortal words: "I think that puppies and kittens are prettier."

This brought down a shower of cross words on my infant head, "unnatural child" being the mildest. Since then, I have learned to be more tactful, and I grew up to have children of my own who, of course, were the most beautiful and the most intelligent babies ever seen! However, I still believe that young creatures in the world of nature are just as appealing and worthy of notice. At Poison Ivy Acres, there are many tiny creatures, and finding one is always a treat because they are not always visible. When I have the chance to share their secret lives, if only for a moment, I look on them with delight.

Once, I was hilling potatoes when my hoe displaced the earth that covered a nest of newborn voles. At least, I think that's what they were. Without identifying colours they could have belonged to several other species of rodent. They were pink, hairless, and blind, and I covered them up quickly. There was no sign of the mother. Had she left the burrow when danger threatened, or, having given birth, had she gone in search of food?

One thing I do know is that there is an exciting world beneath the surface, whether it be the burrows where wild creatures shelter, or treasures waiting to be discovered. Each summer tourists are drawn to the Bonnechere Caves, not far from here. The caves, which nature has carved out of limestone, were formed during the Ordovician period, four million years ago, and were not discovered until the twentieth century. Visitors can see a fine display of Ordovician fossils there.

More recent treasure may be waiting to be found. In 1870, great forest fires blazed in the Upper Ottawa Valley, getting as far as Dow's Lake before being stopped at last. It was this body of water that saved Ottawa from destruction. In Renfrew County, there are many family stories involving valuables that were buried or hidden in wells to save them from the fire and never retrieved. Some day, workmen may come across these items, much as farmers in Britain, while ploughing their fields, have uncovered priceless hoards from the distant past. Our pioneers did not possess gold and jewels, but some of them did have little items that they had brought with them from the old country, treasures that their descendants would love to have.

Amphibians

My treasures are the small creatures that I come across in my daily round. These include various amphibians. Not only do I find them in the wetlands, but they also travel up to the house when the breeding season is passed. On summer nights, I lie in bed listening to the rhythmic croaking of the Bullfrogs and the trill of the Tree Frogs. Sometimes the miniature Tree Frogs climb onto the window screens, where I can admire the lacy grey pattern on their tiny bodies. Then, too, I can observe the orange colouring on the underside of the back legs, something that isn't visible when the frog is seen from above.

I marvel at the great distances that frogs and toads can travel. In summer there is usually a large toad in my vegetable garden, and I wonder how many attempts it has to make before it can get in through the holes of the chain-link fence. I once found and released a very tiny toad that had fallen into an empty flower container. It was leaping into the air with some desperation as it tried to escape from the deep pot, falling back each time, completely exhausted. How long had it taken this little creature to come up from the pond, hopping all the way? It boggles the mind.

Equally small Leopard Frogs often turn up when I'm mowing the lawns, especially the one closest to the pond, and I have to slow down to avoid hitting them as they try to hop out of the way.

On the way up to the gate there is a small pond that lies on the edge of the cedar bush. Each year this pond is home to what sounds like hundreds of Spring Peepers that come out as soon as the ice is gone from the surface, although there was one year when something happened and they were not there. Fortunately, they were heard again the following year.

Spring Peepers are very small frogs that, when fully grown, may measure from three-quarters of an inch to a little over an inch. They call in chorus, and most welcome their music is because it heralds the happy news that we have come safely through the winter and spring is here to stay.

Here is the strange part. When I walk up the lane, I can hear them from a long distance away, but when I come close to their habitat, utter silence falls. A patch of wasteland several yards wide lies between the water and the lane, so there is no way that my footsteps can be heard, especially when I come on tiptoe, and I would not have thought that the ground would have trembled under my feet to such an extent that the frogs could have heard it.

No matter what I do, the frogs freeze at my approach, only to start up again when I've moved on. To my disappointment, I've never seen a Spring Peeper, although I peer into the water through polaroid sunglasses. Other frogs make themselves readily available to me, but not those elusive little peepers. The following are found at Poison Ivy Acres: American Toad (*Bufo americanus*); Northern Leopard Frog (*Rana pipiens*); American Bullfrog (*Rana catesbeiana*); Wood Frog (*Rana sylvatica*); Spring Peeper (*Hyla crucifer*); and Grey Tree Frog (*Hyla versicolor*).

Mice!

I don't like it when a mouse comes into the house! I am not afraid of live mice — in their proper place — but I'm squeamish about dealing with dead ones, and all my cats are good mousers who proudly display their kill for my inspection. Whenever possible, I capture the rodents alive and release them outside, simply because I want to avoid dealing with corpses.

Do you know what I mean when I talk about our setters pointing? When one noticed something of interest, he would stare intently, raising his right front paw. The other dogs would "honour his point" by standing well back, waiting to see what would happen next. Cats also do this, although they don't raise a paw. Many times I have seen one of my cats waiting patiently to attack its prey, while the others crouch some distance behind, alert, yet not prepared to interfere.

I was most surprised when I found myself in the position of main predator, while the cats watched and waited. A small Field Mouse had somehow found its way into my bedroom and was alarmed to find itself the subject of several pairs of eyes. In the manner of such creatures, it failed to retreat to the point of entry, and instead darted uselessly along the top of a chest of drawers. Then the fun started.

Armed with a plastic pail and a corn whisk, I attempted to scoop up the mouse. But it was much quicker than I was. Meanwhile, my largest cat, Blackie Ryan, an accomplished hunter in his own right, sat upright on the bed, watching me with great round eyes. His mouth was open, no doubt in anticipation of the kill, but I could have sworn he was laughing. He made no attempt to come forward, and for that I was thankful.

Finally I had to concede defeat. "All right, Blackie!" I told him. "Siccum!" In one lithe movement he raced over to the chest of drawers and in no time at all the chase was over. At least I'd provided the cats with some entertainment!

MAKING MAPLE SYRUP

For many years, making maple syrup was a rite of spring at Poison Ivy Acres. We always looked forward to doing this. As a rule, the season starts on or about St. Patrick's Day, March 17, although I have seen it beginning as early as mid-February, in a year when the run was poor, and as late as the first week of April. A combination of cold nights and warm days is essential for the sap to run. In this area, when neighbours meet at church, or at the grocery store, the first question is always the same: "Is the sap running yet?"

It was DW's delight to go out, drill in hand, to tap the trees, inserting a spile into each hole and fitting on the buckets and lids. I didn't go with him on those occasions. My job would come at the other end of the season, when it was my task to fit miniature corks into the holes where the spiles had been, and to scrub out the dozens of pails before storing them away. One can have too much of a good thing!

A Sugar Maple has to be at least forty years old before it can be tapped. At the edge of the hardwood bush, we had some gigantic maples that were big enough to take four taps, but we seldom used any of those because they were too far away. If you have ever staggered along with a full pail of sap sloshing over your boots, you will know that accessibility is a prime consideration. Make no mistake about it, making syrup is very hard work!

Most of our Sugar Maples are on the slopes on either side of the lane, and sliding down a hill carrying a full pail of sap is no joke — especially when there is a crust on the snow. I got used to moving cautiously, because for every few steps I took on a solid surface there was one where I sank down suddenly through the crust, barking my shins.

Although there are lids on the pails, a squirrel sometimes worms its way underneath and drowns. Needless to say, that sap is a write-off. Syrup-making involves a lot of muttering and cursing. Commercial producers use pipelines, which take some of the work out of sap-gathering, but these are not feasible for amateurs with sparser bushes. Professional producers also have more sophisticated equipment, including evaporators.

People who grumble about the high cost of maple syrup don't understand that it takes forty gallons of sap to make one gallon of syrup. Even more is called for when maple sugar is the end product. For this reason, we seldom sold our syrup, mostly giving it away to friends. The joy was in the process, which was just as well because any monetary reward can't come close to paying the producer a decent wage. Commercial producers have long been aware of

DW prepares to tap his trees. For countless years, making maple syrup was a rite of spring at Poison Ivy Acres. Sadly, many of the trees were badly damaged during the ice storm of 1996 and have now deteriorated.

this. Many of them supplement their meagre income by operating pancake houses, where patrons can sit down to enjoy a reasonably priced treat.

There are other misconceptions. Numerous friends from the city loved to come out for the day to share in the work, and very welcome they were, too. Sometimes they would arrive on a Saturday, only to find that there was nothing for them to do. Sap does not run continuously. If it had run on Wednesday or Thursday, it would have already been boiled. We had to explain that it could not be kept for days in the gathering tank or it would go sour.

DW took great delight in making his syrup as close to perfection as possible. It had to have the right amount of sugar content if it was to be sold or exhibited at the fall fair. As the boil came close to the end, he would constantly skim off the foam before dipping his thermometer into the syrup. When it had reached the correct temperature, the huge pan had to be pulled off the fire in a hurry. This is not as easy as it sounds. If it doesn't happen fast enough the sugar content will be too high, and one's chances at the fair will be lessened. DW earned many first-place prizes for his maple syrup.

He was particularly proud of his "Extra Light," which is a very pale syrup. Another popular misconception is that very dark syrup is somehow better and sweeter, and some people will feel cheated unless their syrup is almost black. However, as an expert once explained to us, scrupulous cleanliness is necessary to produce the paler varieties. Although the many hours of boiling will kill off any germs, using an ancient open pan which is left unwashed between uses will contribute to the final colour. Attention to such details undoubtedly contributed to DW's annual success at the fair. Or should I say that I had a part in this? My job as handmaiden was to take the pan after every boil to the place near the sugar shack where the spring runoff brings clear water tumbling down to the waterfall, and to scrub away the sticky residue with a stiff brush.

Sometimes in country museums, one can see syrup-making equipment that was used by people in the past. Sap was once collected in wooden troughs, and boiled in huge cauldrons. Spiles, too, have evolved through the years and, although we have used plastic ones more recently, we have a variety of metal ones on hand.

Pioneer women depended on maple syrup and maple sugar for cooking and baking, and those who had a sugar bush on the farm had an advantage over others who did not. Agricultural censuses of the nineteenth century show that huge amounts of syrup were made, with almost unimaginable hours of work involved. Fortunately, many people had large families back then, so extra help was always available.

I have read accounts of early syrup-making among our First Nations people who, of course, were not equipped with metal pails and boiling pans. Apparently the sap was heated by dumping hot rocks into the containers they did possess. Having sat for hours beside a fire, when it seems that the sap will never reach boiling point, I wince when I think of how long it must have taken using the hot-rock method. Can it possibly have been true? And if it was, who did all the work involved? The women, of course. Some things never change.

Even DW became impatient at times. At two o'clock one morning, he came to the house, staggering under the weight of a large pail of half-done syrup. He explained that it would be faster to finish up on my electric cookstove. It was faster, all right. Not being good at multi-tasking, he had returned from doing something else to find that the syrup had bubbled all over the stove and leached down through the oven.

No, I didn't nag. I just disappeared in a hurry and left him to clean up the mess, which, to be fair, he did. As well as possible, that is. I should tell you, though, that if you want to know if your kitchen floor is clean after such an episode, just walk over it in your sock feet. Then you will know the difference!

IN THE HARDWOOD BUSH

In the hardwood bush, there are many hidden treasures in the spring. It is much higher up than the land surrounding the house, and the spring runoff bubbles over the rocks up there, bringing melted snow down from the hayfields and eventually to the creek.

There is a place where fiddleheads grow, and these are a rare treat if they are found and cooked early enough, when they are still tightly coiled. They can be bought in the super-markets locally but, like most produce, there is a great difference between freshly picked fiddleheads and those that have travelled a long way, not reaching the consumer until they are fairly well-advanced in age. The fiddlehead is actually the top of the Ostrich Fern, which grows abundantly in this part of the township.

Another delicious product of the hardwood bush is a darker Morel (*Morchella augus-ticeps*). I was quite surprised when an American visitor appeared at the door one spring morning, asking permission to go up to the bush to seek out these mushrooms. Apparently, when he was a boy he had stayed with his grandparents who lived two miles from Poison Ivy Acres, and they had come here to pick the Morels. These people and their friends, the family who owned this property at the time, were descendants of Prussian settlers, and I understand that Morels had been especially popular in the old country.

The greatest treasure of all that the hardwood bush affords usually blooms a little later than these choice edibles. This is the Yellow Lady's Slipper (*Cypripedium calceolus*), a beautiful member of the orchid family. I think of it as the moccasin flower, because of the shape of the flowers, although I believe that this name is more often applied to the Pink Lady's Slipper, a species that doesn't grow on the property.

The Audubon Society Field Guide to North American Wildflowers explains that American Indians made a medicine from the roots of the Yellow Lady's Slipper, which they drank as a treatment for worms. *Too much information,* I thought. *More than I want to know, really!* I prefer to gaze on this plant because of its rare beauty.

I usually see at least three clumps of these flowers in the bush, including numerous "moccasins." I would never dream of picking them or digging them up, but in any case, I have read that they do not transplant well. It is sufficient to make an annual pilgrimage to the hardwood bush to gaze down at them, while reflecting on the infinite variety of all that is part of nature.

One autumn morning, walking with the dogs along the outer fringes of the bush, I had my first and only sighting of a Wood Frog. It was so well camouflaged that if it had not moved slightly, I wouldn't have noticed it at all. If you have ever shuffled your way through piles of fallen maple leaves, when they have curled up at the edges and their colour has changed to a pinkish brown, you will be able to visualize the colour of this tiny amphibian.

The size of the adult Wood Frog varies from one and half to three inches. During the spring breeding season this creature, like other frogs, is found in woodland ponds and pools, but later in the year it moves to the woods, where it is barely distinguishable among the leaves on the forest floor. I'm sure that the Wood Frog is far more common here than I know, although I'm sure that — if I were so inclined — I could spend weeks scrabbling among the leaves without ever catching a glimpse of one.

So many of my encounters with wildlife have come quite by chance, and I know how fortunate I am to spend most of my time here in the country, where I can share in the secret lives of other species.

THE CLIMBING SNAKE

Thirty years ago, we had a conservatory, or greenhouse, built on to the house, with the idea of filling it with lots of lovely plants. We also intended to raise tomatoes and peppers from seed, to give us a head start on the gardening season. Unfortunately, it was difficult to regulate the temperature out there, and after we came home from a trip to find that a house-sitter had managed to let everything die, we lost interest. The room became a repository for plant pots and other garden paraphernalia.

Later, part of this was sectioned off with chain-link fencing. In wintertime, the dogs stayed in the house when we left for short periods, but Rusty, who suffered from separation anxiety, couldn't be trusted not to tear the place apart. When it was too cold for him to go to the outside pen, the greenhouse was the next best thing. He could look through the picture window into the kitchen to keep an eye on his housemates, which seemed to offer him some consolation.

There is a small drainage hole to the outside that is still useful because the table can be sluiced off after jobs involving potting soil have taken place. On rare occasions this hole serves as a doorway for a large milk snake, which seems to want to use the greenhouse as a place to shed its skin. I can't say I enjoy having my territory invaded this way, but there it is. I enjoy observing snakes in the wild, but I don't care to have them in the house!

An Eastern Milk Snake faces down the camera. Non-venomous and beneficial to people, these snakes are good mousers.

The snake climbs to a high shelf and begins the process there. When it is all over, the creature returns to the outside world, leaving the skin hanging down. Not having watched it in action, I do wonder exactly how this happens.

One day, I noticed Ruby crouching on the kitchen table, gazing upwards in horror at something near the ceiling of the greenhouse. I followed her gaze, and, sure enough, there was the snake, about to make its way to the shelves at the other end of the room. It had to go! I suppose that the vibrations made when I opened the door and thumped on the wall made the snake decide to leave for safer quarters. I watched in fascinated horror as it began to descend the chain-link divider. Although I was squeamish, I couldn't help admiring the way in which this happened.

The rear end of the snake was bent over like a hook and fastened around the metal link. Keeping this in place, it slowly worked its way downwards. This was a very large, bulky snake, but somehow it managed to stretch itself into a long length no thicker than my little finger. I must admit to being most impressed by this feat! Nature had provided the snake with a useful compensation for being born without arms or legs. I am beginning to wonder what else snakes can do that I don't know about.

The episode reminded me of another interesting experience I once had with a water snake. I was canoeing down the creek when a large snake approached me, travelling in the opposite direction. It was bobbing along with its head held well above the water, and somehow I felt that it was feeling quite joyful about its expedition that day. Rusty watched it go by with some interest, turning his doggy face up to me as if to say, "There! Wasn't that a pretty sight?" And I had to agree that it was.

A CLUTCH OF EGGS

In summertime, I make a low fence around the two upper lawns by placing cedar rails on pieces of log. Having to move these aside is a bit of a nuisance when I have to mow the grass, but it's worth it. I like the way it looks and it also protects the lawns, which I've spent years reclaiming from the wild. It may only be field grass, but it's upsetting when people drive over the lawns in wet weather, leaving large gouges behind.

Sometimes I find small creatures under the logs, but my most interesting find was a clutch of good-sized oval, white eggs. *What could they be?* I wondered. Not long before this a neighbour had been helping me unload firewood nearby, and she had uncovered a beautiful Blue-spotted Salamander. Could the little lizard or another one like it have put the eggs there? But no, I doubted whether it could have squeezed between the piece of log and the ground.

On the other hand, when I had turned the logs over I had disturbed a garter snake under one, and a Dekay's Little Brown Snake beneath another. Knowing that some snakes lay eggs while others produce live young, I decided to find out more.

Having taken part in a herpetofaunal survey for two years on Poison Ivy Acres, I knew that there are at least six species of snake here, all of which are harmless, and beneficial to people, since they feed on garden pests. Twenty-three species of snake are native to Canada, of which I have the following: Dekay's Little Brown Snake, Northwestern Garter Snake, Smooth Green Snake, Eastern Milk Snake, Northern Red-bellied Snake, and Northern Water Snake.

I felt that I could rule out the water snake, which I've never seen on the lawn. I did find one stretched out in a flower bed once, looking like a length of old garden hose. Now it was a question of looking up the rest in Barbara Froom's *The Snakes of Ontario*. I learned that the garter snake produces live young, as do the Red-bellied Snake and the Little Brown Snake. This narrowed it down to the Eastern Milk Snake and the reclusive Smooth Green Snake. I have often seen the latter on these lawns, whereas the milk snake favours a more sheltered terrain, so it is possible that these were the eggs of the Smooth Green Snake. Eggs have been laid in this same location in other years, but they are usually found and eaten by skunks.

Not being an expert in these matters, I have come to no reliable conclusion as to what had laid the clutch of eggs I found. The only way to know for sure is to find the young snakes after they have hatched out, and I shall watch for this in the future. In the meantime, this has been a fascinating exercise.

 # THE DESTROYING ANGEL

I usually experience a frisson of excitement when I find something in nature that is new to me, or something with which I'm already familiar but seldom get to see. So it was when a "destroying angel" suddenly appeared on the lawn behind the house. No, I hadn't been tasting magic mushrooms, which certainly don't grow at Poison Ivy Acres! This was an *Amanita*

virosa, a member of the family that includes the world's most poisonous mushrooms. It is commonly called the Destroying Angel.

I expect that most people could identify the *Amanita muscaria*, that pretty white-dotted red mushroom that is often shown in children's picture books with a frog or a fairy perched on top. Referred to as a toadstool, which is the layperson's expression for a poisonous fungus, it is well-known to be dangerous. We do have those here, but its relative, the Destroying Angel, is the deadliest of all.

The Audubon Field Guide to North American Mushrooms describes the *Amanita virosa* as one of the most strikingly beautiful of all our mushrooms, and certainly this one looked innocent and lovely, standing alone near the base of a Bur Oak. Its habitat and the fact that it was alone alerted me to what it was.

In my imagination I felt that it contained some hidden menace, but that was only because I knew it for what it was. I had experienced a similar feeling of horror when standing on the deck of a ship one November morning, gazing at an iceberg that wasn't far away. Who could ever forget the voyage of the *Titanic*? Of course we were not in any danger and the captain had alerted us to the

The Destroying Angel. This is the deadliest mushroom here and must be handled with care.

iceberg's presence, suggesting that his passengers might like to observe one close up. Such is the power of suggestion. Even so, that iceberg had a frightening greenish glow about it that made it appear evil in its own right.

There is no mistake about the death-dealing potential of that white *amanita*, though: it is a killer. This shiny white mushroom may be seen at any time between June and November. It has a stem that may grow as tall as eight inches, and a cap that may be flat or convex. It has pale, white gills that are not attached to the stem, and, before it opens, this mushroom is completely enclosed in an outer membrane or veil, which eventually breaks. The membrane remains at the base of the stem as a sort of cup.

The spore print of the *Amanita virosa* is white, but so are the spore prints of many other mushrooms. Take great care if you decide to make a print of this specimen; wash your hands thoroughly after handling it. It isn't necessary to eat this mushroom in order to become ill.

Like me, you may be delighted to get a glimpse of this pretty thing. Play it safe and take a photo, or make a sketch, just to prove to yourself and others that you have seen it. Remember, this is a fallen angel that can destroy you, given the chance.

MORELS GALORE

Finding morels is a most satisfactory experience, and we have three different varieties of them at Poison Ivy Acres, all edible, as well as at least one species of false morel. Each spring, when the purple violets bloom on the edge of the lane, I know that morel season has come. First of all, the false morels appear, usually during the first week of May, and about a week later the true morels can be found. True morels look something like an odd-shaped brain, while the false variety are ugly looking blobs of black or brown. Judging by the colour plates in Orson K. Miller Junior's *Mushrooms of North America*, the false morels I've found here may be the common *Gyromitra californica*, or possibly the *Gyromitra infula*. I have not been able to determine if those species do in fact grow here.

However, I don't find it necessary to make a positive identification because, generally speaking, all false morels should be avoided like the plague. They carry toxins that are poisonous. It so happens that one or two of the *Gyromitras* are, in fact, edible, but I strongly advise readers not to taste them except on the advice of an experienced mycologist, a mushroom expert. I am definitely not among their number and the possibility of error is too great to take chances.

False morels can cause severe gastrointestinal distress, as a friend of DW's found out the hard way when he fried some for breakfast. He came down with an unpleasant flu-like illness, although fortunately he soon recovered. Cases of death have been known. I've heard that the early German settlers in our county used to eat them, but in their case the fungi were boiled until, apparently, the bad effect was minimized. Or perhaps they could tell the difference between one species and another?

A false morel. These appear about a week before the edible variety, and should not be eaten.

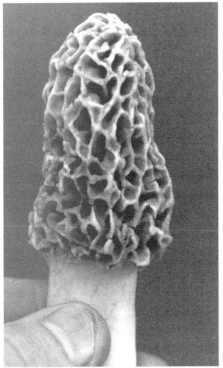

LEFT: *A delicious morel (*Morchella esculenta*), which appears at Poison Ivy Acres in May.*

RIGHT: *An excellent find! A good selection of morels!*

By contrast, true morels are delicious. On one part of the property, we have the pale brown *Morchella esculenta*, and on another, the darker *Morchella augusticeps*. Occasionally I have found the *Morchella deliciosa* and the *Morchella libera*. These vary in taste, with the *esculenta* being the choicest. Most of the time there are just a few in one place, but there was one never-to-be-forgotten spring when I gathered a bushel basket full of them, all from one small area.

We invited a group of friends in to sample these delights and I was kept busy cooking the morels, which I had cut in half lengthwise and sautéed in butter and lemon juice. These pieces were served on slivers of homemade whole-wheat bread. I had prepared a big pot of vegetable soup to serve to anyone who didn't fancy the mushrooms, but it wasn't touched. The morels were too popular!

After that, DW always joked that I was able to sniff out morels, just as a pig does truffles, even though he scoffed at the idea that they have a scent. In vain, I tried to convince him that they do indeed have a strong odour, which I can identify from some distance away.

 # IN SEARCH OF MUSHROOMS

Finding mushrooms can be just as exciting as spotting an uncommon bird or meeting a seldom-seen animal, and Poison Ivy Acres is a great environment for fungi. At different times of year, especially after a period of rain, they appear in great variety. Even their names have a certain ring to them.

Morels, Chanterelles, *Amanitas,* Russulas, Parasols, Boletes, Coprinus, Shaggy Manes, Bracket Fungus, Coral Mushrooms, Cup Fungi, and many more have been found here. Polypores occur in various colours, growing on trees. Most are edible, or at least non-poisonous, when they are fresh, but they harden quickly and become woody. I have also found Jelly Fungi, Puffballs, Earth Stars, and Stink Horns.

At one time, DW embarked on a project of listing and tasting most of the mushrooms found here, which of course involved careful testing to make sure that we didn't eat any poisonous varieties. Spore prints were made by placing mushroom caps on black paper, gills down, and I was surprised to learn that these prints can appear in different colours: white, lilac, green, pink, yellow, brown, or black! He compared each specimen with its salient features: shape, colour, rings, with or without gills, etc. In addition to this, each one was photographed, which resulted in a large number of colour slides.

A delicious Parasol Mushroom, the Lepiota procera.

LEFT: *The* Pleurotus ostreatus *or Oyster Mushroom grows on trees here. Although edible when young, it soon becomes hard like wood.*

RIGHT: *The reverse of the Oyster Mushroom, showing its gills.*

We acquired several very good books filled with colour illustrations. But without a doubt, the best reference book for our purposes was *The Mushroom Trail Guide* by Phyllis Glick, which describes each mushroom according to its parts. No tasting was done until DW was confident that the mushroom in question was fit to eat. We soon found that many of the fungi found here, while edible, are less than tasty. That is, they are useful to know about if one happened to be lost or living off the land, but they are not what one would choose to bring to the table when other food is available.

Being less adventurous, I stick to a different form of knowledge. I have learned where on the property certain choice varieties are likely to be found and the time of year when they appear, and I'm happy to observe them. Sometimes I photograph them, or make sketches. As for eating them, my favourites are the various morels and the Parasol Mushrooms, such as the *Lepiota procera*. Chanterelles, which grow in the bush across the creek, are considered by many people to be choice, but in my estimation they are overrated. If they are not picked soon enough they are taken over by small white worms, which is off-putting, to say the least.

Going out into the woods to look for mushrooms can be a most interesting hobby, especially if you want to build a photograph collection. Please do not taste any of them unless you have proof of what they are, and do not take anything I have said here as an invitation to do so. As I said earlier, I am an interested amateur, not a trained mycologist.

While not all mushrooms are dangerous, and only a few can actually have lethal results, there are some which can give you some nasty surprises. Take the family of Inky Caps, for instance. Several species are common at Poison Ivy Acres. The Shaggy Mane (*Coprinus comatus*) is edible and choice. The *Coprinus micaceus* is edible, but not great tasting. The *Coprinus atramentarius* is edible, but it shouldn't be consumed with or after an alcoholic drink. A toxic reaction can occur and you may soon feel very sick indeed.

WILDFLOWERS OF POISON IVY ACRES

If William Shakespeare could come back to life, he would feel right at home at Poison Ivy Acres, where there are numerous flowers and birds that would seem familiar to him. A study of his plays reveals that he was an accomplished naturalist, not in the sense of one who takes up flower identification and birding as a hobby, but as a countryman who was familiar with the natural world around him.

I have some fascinating booklets that were compiled by Dr. Levi Fox, director of the Shakespeare Birthplace Trust at Stratford-upon-Avon. One of these deals with Shakespeare's flowers, the other with Shakespeare's birds. Citing chapter and verse in each case, Dr. Fox shows that the Bard's plays contain numerous references to living things in the countryside. There are forty-six references involving twenty-three flowers and fifteen herbs. Twenty-nine birds are referred a total of seventy-three times.

"When the wind is southerly I know a hawk from a handsaw," Hamlet says, in Act II, Scene 2 (a handsaw is an old name for a heron). It is obvious that Shakespeare knew what he was talking about where nature was concerned. A number of the birds he wrote about inhabit Poison Ivy Acres, although many of them are a different species within the same genus.

Similarly, a few of the flowers and herbs that he knew can also be found in Canada, although many are now domesticated varieties. Dr. Fox suggests that Shakespeare's marigolds and winking mary-buds were not the garden flower we know today, but the Marsh Marigold, or king-cup, which flourish on marshy ground. This is the very first flower to bloom on my property in the spring. Marsh Marigolds, also known as Mary flowers, can be seen in ditches around the township early in the spring.

Long ago, we transplanted some beside the tiny pond near the sugar shack, which have multiplied in the intervening years. This wet place is fed by the spring runoff and, unless we have heavy rains during the year, it sometimes dries up in summer. At winter's end, I can see the marigold plants coming to life underneath the ice and, knowing that the flowers will shortly appear, I marvel that so tender and juicy a plant can survive under such conditions.

Wildflowers abound at Poison Ivy Acres. Some are fairly common from year to year, while others appear as if by magic, to be admired, recorded, and never to be seen again. All of them reflect the changing seasons, and they flourish or fail according to the weather. The smaller flowers herald the coming of spring. The first to appear is the Spring Beauty and then the Hepaticas, the latter so-called because the shape of their leaves resembles a liver. Most are a deep mauve, but sometimes I find a flower that is pink or white.

Soon afterwards, we find small yellow or mauve violets and much larger, deep purple ones. Then the Snow Trilliums can be found, followed by the large variety some time later, and sometimes by the dark red Wakerobin, which is yet another trillium. DW once found Painted Trilliums in the Pontiac, but so far, to our disappointment, they have never shown themselves here.

The delicate Trout Lily (known locally as the Dog-toothed Violet) is here in profusion, as well as others of the lily family, the columbines and lady's slippers. Dandelions soon lift their smiling faces to the sun. Why do gardeners dislike them so much? All their parts are edible, a true gift from nature. I have enjoyed many a feast of their young leaves. The pioneers roasted their roots to make a sort of coffee.

Summer brings many colourful flowers, including the Purple Bellflower and the Spotted Touch-me-not. The gentians appear later, both the pretty mauve-fringed variety and the sturdy purple Bottle Gentian. The goldenrods come at a time when the whole countryside turns yellow and green, before the foliage starts to turn colour. Many people believe, mistakenly, that this plant causes allergies, but this is not the case. The culprit is ragweed, which appears at approximately the same time. One of my early childhood memories involves going with my mother to a flower shop, where she purchased long sprays of goldenrod. She arranged them in two tall, green pottery vases that stood on the floor in front of the fireplace in our home. I thought that this was the last word in elegance!

There are more than sixty varieties of goldenrod in North America, and, deciding to make a study of them one summer, I found five of them here. They may look alike from a distance, but a closer examination shows many differences in their structure, as you will find out from studying the field guides. The summer of 2009 was so wet that the goldenrod plants reached a towering height of six feet, and they spread like wildfire, to the detriment of the pasture land.

There are several good flower guides to be had. My favourite is the *Field Guide to Wildflowers* by Roger Tory Peterson and Margaret McKenny. The sections of the book are arranged by colour, which is very helpful for anyone finding a flower new to them, without knowing where to start the process of identification. Once a look-alike plant has been found, one can then concentrate on the shape of the leaves and the arrangement of the flowers on the stem.

The Audubon Society Field Guide to North American Wildflowers is also beautifully done, but the former book suits me better because text and illustrations are found on the same page. In the latter, I find that fumbling back and forth between the picture pages and the texts is a bit of a nuisance, and I sometimes have to use a magnifying glass on the type. However, when in doubt it is always wise to consult more than one source. For a list of wildflowers found at Poison Ivy Acres, see Appendix C.

THE USEFUL TREE

Trees. What an important role they play in my life! Because I live in the bush, I'm surrounded by thousands of them. They provide me with shade in summer, and, in bad weather, they help to shelter me from the storm.

My house is made from logs, cut down by pioneers as long ago as the 1850s. Other log buildings, now adapted to modern use, were also built by those who came before — a horse stable and cow byre, a calf pen, and a granary. A bigger barn, where neighbours sometimes came to dance, has gone now, but the mow logs live on as part of my living-room ceiling. Those settlers depended on trees to provide them with shelter, warmth, furniture, tools, wagons, buckets, and fences, even for food. In turn, the wood was used by coopers, wheelwrights, cabinetmakers, and coffin makers.

Some older people refer to the swamp willows that grow along the creek as "sally trees." They may not know it, but the name comes from the Latin, *Salix canadensis*. This is reflected in an Irish song, "Down by the Sally Gardens." In Ireland, a sally garden was a growth of willows that was reserved for use in thatching roofs.

When the settlers first came, much of the land here was forested with white pine. Along with the lumbering days, this has gone from the scene, and softwoods have taken their place at Poison Ivy Acres. Some venerable hardwoods still remain. Years ago, DW cut down a Red

Oak, which was such a tree. I counted more than 250 rings, which meant that it began grow-ing long before the first Europeans ventured into the district. Our neighbour, Ambrose, felled a large Bur Oak for me when it was in danger of keeling over and blocking the lane. It was hollow, and had housed a large porcupine one winter, but the stump was solid enough, and in that case I counted some two hundred rings.

The trees remind me of the changing seasons. When the poplars up on the hill become shaded with yellow, like a wash added to a watercolour painting, my spirits lift knowing that spring is almost here. When the leaves of the Sugar Maples turn red, the beauty of it is almost too much to bear.

I remember a little girl I once met in Ireland. "Isn't that a scent to make your heart break?" she asked, thrusting a perfume bottle under my nose. And, yes, the changing leaves are a sight to make the heart break, for many reasons. One is made sharply aware of one's own mortality on a crisp autumn morning, however beautiful it may be.

As a keen birdwatcher, I'm thankful for trees that provide shelter, and, in some cases, food for the birds I like to observe. As a writer, I respect the reams of paper I use: trees were sacrificed to provide me with this necessity, as well as the books I like to read.

Trees! How could I survive without them?

DECEMBER

December at Poison Ivy Acres always brings with it memories of Christmases past. These inevitably have something to do with trees. For years, I went out to the bush to pick out a suitable Christmas tree, a task that called for some deliberation. I always tried to choose one that would, in time, have been crowded out by nearby trees or juniper bushes, rather than a free-standing one which should be left to grow to maturity.

My favourite species is the Balsam Fir. A good many of these grow on the edge of the hardwood bush, shielded from the elements by their stronger neighbours. Having cut down the tree with my trusty handsaw, I would drag it home, accompanied by the gambol-ling dogs. Despite the fact that they knew where it had come from, the tree was the object of much curiosity on their part when it was brought inside and stood in a pail of water. Sometimes a sharp "No!" was required when a dog so far forgot himself as to treat the tree as a comfort station.

The year when Ginger and Smokey were still young kittens called for a change in plan. They were thrilled with this new toy, and climbed the branches enthusiastically. In no time at all, the tree was lying flat on the flagstones with the gleeful cats clawing at the greenery. It was put back into place with a thin wire holding it to the wall. The great thing about a log house is that a convenient nail can be hammered in wherever necessary.

Our pretty glass baubles were put away and non-breakable ornaments used instead. The cats delighted in patting the colourful balls, which they obviously thought had been hung for their benefit. Shards of glass on the floor would have been dangerous to the six resident fur persons, not to mention the people who were in the habit of padding about in their sock feet.

Soon after we moved permanently to Poison Ivy Acres, five spruce trees were planted close to the house, three on the south side and two on the west. Those on the south side were meant to keep the house cool in summer, but nowadays they tower over the house, helping to keep out the cold in winter as well. Those on the west side provide a shield from the prevailing winds. Seeing them as they are now, perhaps fifty feet high, I find it hard to believe that I was once able to decorate them with Christmas-tree lights with a star on the top!

All these spruce trees provide excellent shelter for the birds coming to the feeders. There was one unforgettable spring when a grouse laid her eggs at the base of the tallest one. How she managed to raise a family in that spot, when the raccoons were being fed only a few feet away, is a mystery, but it did happen.

Once the snow has arrived, I often wake up in the morning to find that the deer have wandered around close to the house, feeding during the night hours. In December, it is still possible to scrape the snow aside to get at the grass underneath, or to uncover frozen vetch. The deer have not yet been reduced to eating cedar bark, which constitutes their winter diet.

One year my toddler granddaughter, Sarah, and her parents were here for the holidays. On Christmas Eve I took her outside to show her the tracks in the snow. Her eyes lit up when I explained that they were deer tracks.

"Is it Wudolph?" she wanted to know.

"Well, perhaps it was his cousin," I suggested, knowing that she was too young for a lecture on the difference between caribou and White-tailed Deer. She was thrilled, and went into the house to share the news.

"Wudolph's cousin was here!" she told her daddy, beaming with excitement. A hoofprint in the snow is worth a thousand words. So was the fragment of caribou antler on the wall, a souvenir of one of DW's canoe trips in the Canadian North. All that was missing was Santa Claus himself.

THE ICE STORM

The great ice storm of 1996 was an event at Poison Ivy Acres. As I was later to learn, the hydro was off over a wide area of eastern Ontario and western Quebec, as trees and power lines were downed by the weight of the ice. People living in city apartments became refugees in church halls and community centres. Hardware stores quickly ran out of batteries and lanterns, and generators were in great demand.

None of this particularly affected me at Poison Ivy Acres, as I'm always well prepared for winter, with batteries, candles, and so on. Starting in September, I stock up on tinned food and pet supplies. I don't really like canned goods, but it's always a good idea to hold some in reserve. When the power is off for two or three days — something that happens in the country at least twice a year — frozen food rapidly defrosts, and even though I do buy so-called fresh produce when I go to town every ten days or so, it only lasts for a short time.

Hydro workers were seconded to the area from different parts of the province, and the army was called in to assist. Deep in the bush I knew nothing of this, but as the days wore on and the temperature dropped to thirty below, extra measures were called for here. I shut off most of the house, retreating to the living room and kitchen. The daylight hours were spent bringing in wood by the toboggan load for the kitchen stove and the big fireplace in the living room, and melting snow and ice to provide myself and the dogs with water.

I moved a bed into the living room, placing it as close to the fireplace as I dared. I invariably woke up at 4:00 a.m. to find that the fire had gone out, and then, reluctant to leave my warm nest, I had to struggle up to get it going again, with my teeth chattering as I waited for it to ignite. One morning, I woke up to find Ginger curled up on my head. It's a well-known fact that we lose a certain amount of body heat through our heads, and apparently the cat had found this out for himself and decided to take advantage of the extra warmth.

The house is built into the side of a hill, which means that the path past my kitchen window is on a slope. In a normal winter I put wood ashes on this path to make it safe to walk on, but that year I had better things to do. I had to smile when I glanced out to see Jordie sliding past, unable to stop until he reached the back door. He was thankful to get back inside, to cozy up to the meagre heat.

While meals could be cooked on the wood stove during the day, working by candlelight was annoying, so I took to baking potatoes in the ashes in the fireplace. I celebrated my January birthday by eating a lunch of peanut butter sandwiches, washed down by melted snow. The dogs and cats, of course, had their usual canned food and dry kibble, so nothing was different for them. I don't know how the wild creatures fared. Birds arrived to eat the seeds I put out, but everything in the country was covered with a layer of ice, so I'm sure that many animals and birds suffered badly.

By some miracle, the telephone still worked even though the lines were so badly stretched as to be just a few feet above the ground. Of course, there were no cellphones here back then; not that they would have helped, since there is no service here to this day. Friends were able to check on me to see if I was all right, and my mother succeeded in placing a transatlantic call to wish me many happy returns of the day.

When the power was restored in town, a friend offered me a place to stay, a kind suggestion which I turned down. No doubt, I could have got away on snowshoes to meet a car at the road, but I couldn't leave my animals alone to suffer, nor did I want to leave the house without heat. By some miracle, the pipes didn't freeze, and for that I was thankful.

After nine days, power was restored to Poison Ivy Acres. Other parts of the township had received it much earlier. Kind neighbours arrived with chainsaws to cut up the many trees that had fallen across the lane, and, at last, after sixteen days, I was able to get out.

The worst part, for me, had involved being unable to get out walking for all that time. Now I rather nervously hiked up to the gate, hoping not to slip and fall. The trees were still creaking ominously, so I wore a hard hat, and there was a constant *ping ping ping* as small icicles bounced off it as I picked my way along. The sad result of nature's fury was that our beautiful sugar bush suffered badly. Over the past decade many of them have deteriorated, becoming favourite nesting places for woodpeckers before finally succumbing to the inevitable.

During the nine days when I had to work day and night just to survive, I reflected on the experience of the early pioneers, who had to undergo this misery for six months of every year. It must have been particularly hard on those people who had come from the British Isles, where the climate is much milder than in Canada.

The people who had inhabited Poison Ivy Acres before DW purchased it had managed without power, but even so they were better equipped than I was during the storm. A hand-operated pump provided water, and I'm told that a network of pipes extended from their wood stove to heat the whole house, which at that time covered what is now my living room and kitchen. They used oil lamps for lighting, and they were snug in winter. It seems that sometimes the old ways were best.

When power was finally restored, many stories emerged in connection with the ice storm. There were heartwarming tales of neighbour helping neighbour, of people going the extra mile to help strangers, and the occasional stories of heroism. Then, too, we heard about those people without conscience who burgled unoccupied homes whose shivering inhabitants had taken refuge in temporary shelters. Some people stole generators, while others charged greatly inflated prices for performing cleanup services. It seems that troubled times bring out the best in mankind, as well as the worst. The great ice storm of 1996 was proof of that.

ANOTHER ICE STORM

On Christmas Eve 2009, I didn't pay much attention when the CBC meteorologist announced that an ice storm was heading for the Ottawa Valley. I assumed he meant a short-lived event with ice pellets or freezing rain, rather than a replay of the great ice storm of 1996. There were to be no comings or goings at Poison Ivy Acres over the holidays, so there was no need for me to worry.

On Christmas Day, I brought in a supply of firewood. Then I filled a large pot and several bottles with water, and went to bed, confident that I was well prepared. I woke up on Boxing Day to find that the power had been off in the night for a couple of hours, but it had apparently been restored around 2:00 a.m. Fortified with hot coffee, I tried to open my office window to throw out seeds for the birds, but it was frozen shut. I had to go outside to feed them, and that was when I discovered a crust on the ice, which broke under my feet. It would not be a good day for the wild animals that depend on catching small creatures for their food, I thought, remembering the winter of the Red Fox.

Sunday, December 27, was the day of our annual bird count. I looked out that morning to see a silvery wilderness. The lilacs were bending over as if to kiss the ground, and the tiny branches of the Amur Maple shone silver under a thick layer of ice. Across the valley, the trees were weighed down with snow, held in place by a crusting of ice. A watery sun came out and illuminated a shining wasteland where the lawn sloped down to the pond.

Would I be able to take part in the count, I wondered, *or would I have to resign myself to staying in to enumerate the birds who came to the feeders?* For years I used to drive around my designated area, stopping at intervals to do a few miles on foot. These days I put my car away for the winter, so I'm assigned to work at Poison Ivy Acres, and to go on foot along the township roads near the property.

I was concerned that I might not be able to get up the steep hill on the lane, so I set out rather gingerly, hoping not to slip and fall. I need not have worried. The cleats on my boots and the spikes on my hike poles made snapping sounds with every step I took, but this ice was nothing like the hard stuff we usually get when a freeze-up follows a January thaw.

I travelled through an avenue of bowed-down, ice-laden trees. Cedars and pines drooped close to the ground, and hundreds of Ironwood saplings were bent double. The Sugar Maples, denuded of their leaves, had withstood the storm, but for how long? They were already damaged from the storm of 1996, which most of them had barely managed to survive.

Despite the early hour, the township roads were well-sanded, but the trip was a waste of time. A lone raven flying overhead and a Northern Shrike sitting in a tree were the only birds to be seen. Having peered up uselessly into several cedar trees to see if any Wild Turkeys were roosting there, I turned for home. The usual birds were waiting for me there. Blue Jays, Black-capped Chickadees, White-breasted Nuthatches, Downy and Hairy Woodpeckers, and Tree Sparrows. A large flock of American Goldfinches, which had been with me all week, were still there, but a beautiful pair of Purple Finches was missing. They returned the next day, too late to be included in the count. A bonus was the sudden appearance of three Pine Siskins. Having not seen any for a while, I was delighted to see these small brown birds with their yellow wing patches.

It was then that I had my first experience of ice fog. A blanket of mist swirled up over the creek, and in minutes it was impossible to see over the valley. I had heard of this phenomenon on the news a few days earlier, when it had caused a seventy-car pileup in Ottawa. Within an hour the fog had gone again, as mysteriously as it had come. I decided that this was the strangest bird count day I'd known in forty years.

After lunch, I went out again and, having headed to a spot where I hoped to find Wild Turkeys, I was pleased to find eighteen of them running across a field. A few crows and Blue Jays were the only other birds to make an appearance. The trees on either side of the road were shedding their burden of ice, and I found myself walking over piles of finger-sized pieces that littered the ground. Being soft, these were no problem for me, but as I later heard, the ice was less kind to those of my fellow birders who were cautiously driving around the area in small cars.

Back at Poison Ivy Acres, I found that nothing had changed. The trees were still shrouded in ice, and they remained so until the middle of January. Most of my land is made up of hills and valleys, and the house is far below the level of the nearest township road. The temperature here is usually about five degrees lower than it is up there, and I have been known to have my vegetables destroyed by a midsummer frost while my neighbours' gardens are still doing well.

I can foresee that many of my trees and shrubs will have suffered damage during this short ice storm of 2009, but even so, we were fortunate here. Thousands of people in eastern Ontario and the Outaouais were without power for more than twenty-four hours. The awesome power of nature had been at work again.

 # TRACKS IN THE SNOW

I could hardly believe my eyes when I was walking up the lane one morning. The snowbanks were covered with minuscule black, hopping objects that looked like fleas! I was used to seeing various hopping creatures in summer, but this was something new. What were they doing, out in the cold like that? What exactly were they? Were they harmful, in the same way that mosquitoes and black flies feast on humans? Might they infest the dogs' coats? I resolved to find out.

A search of my field guides helped me identify them as Snow Fleas, otherwise known as a species of Springtails, insects that breed in leaf litter in moist woodlands. I was glad to learn that Springtails rarely occur as pests, for the fleas I saw were too numerous to count.

That was some years ago, and I haven't seen any since. My field guide states that there may be millions of these little insects in a single acre, which makes me wonder why I haven't seen more of them. I'm sure that an etymologist would know these things, but it remains a mystery to me. Still, I was pleased to have added something new to my life list.

I am better able to unravel the little mysteries that appear on my lane in the form of bird and animal tracks. Each day, when I start off on my two-mile round trip to pick up the mail, I see that many such creatures have adopted this private road as their own thoroughfare. Wolves, coyotes, foxes, Snowshoe Hares, and Red Squirrels travel it frequently, as do raccoons. Grouse and Wild Turkey prints show where those birds have hunted for food.

Occasionally, a story will be recorded in the snow. A little pile of feathers will be all that remains of a bird that has been captured and eaten by a hawk. Tiny rodent tracks, overlaid by the marks made by the wingtips of a bird, possibly an owl, attest to a successful hunt for food.

These tracks in the snow, many of them freshly made each day, tell me that I share Poison Ivy Acres with a great many wild creatures, and this is good to know. Days may pass without any rare sightings, although the more common birds and animals are always visible nearby. The tracks reassure me that many animals and birds are constantly on the move, even when I don't see them. This is exciting because it means that I never know what might happen next. In the world of nature, there is always something to look forward to.

One very windy day in February, I encountered snow flurries as I hiked out for the mail. By the time I reached the gate on the return journey, there was a complete whiteout. Visibility was nil, and if I hadn't known the road so well, there is no doubt that I would have become disoriented. As it was, I plodded along with my head down, wanting to get home as soon as possible.

The footprints I had made on the way out were completely obliterated, even though I had made them less than half an hour earlier. When I emerged into an open spot on the lane, I was interested to see fresh tracks where a wolf had crossed in my absence. Apparently, I had missed it by inches, as the saying goes. It had gone into the cedar bush, probably seeking shelter from the nasty weather, although, being closer to the ground than a human, the wind may have bothered it less than it did me.

Scurrying along the final quarter mile that led home, I felt a lifting of the spirit. Once again, I had come across something of interest in the wild, and I felt all the better for having done so.

RUNNING AHEAD

At the end of my property there is a country road that I use as a shortcut on my way to church. My end of this narrow, unpaved road, with its many twists and turns, is not maintained in winter because there are no longer people living on the old farms nearby. Long ago, there were settlers there, but it was difficult to make a living on the rocky land, which is part of the Laurentian Shield. Over time the families died out or moved on. Their dwelling places are mainly used as hunt camps now.

One Sunday morning, I had just turned my car onto this road when I found my way barred by a large bear. It looked at me for a long moment before giving a snort of disgust and turning away. Then it ambled off, with my vehicle following slowly behind it. Soon the bear picked up speed and I adjusted accordingly, but the road is so narrow that I couldn't get past. Honking the horn did no good. The animal kept trundling along, determined not

*Bunny races through
the spring floodwater
at the bottom of the
steep hill that visi-
tors like to ski down.
Not everyone makes
it safely to the creek
without coming to grief.*

to give way. Luckily there is a fork in the road about three miles from home, where the bear was able to peel off, and I continued along "the road not taken."

That bear could have plunged into the ditch along the way, or disappeared into a wooded area, but it chose not to. *Why was this?* I wondered. I have seen this sort of behaviour by wild creatures many times before. I often meet grouse or Wild Turkeys wandering on my lane, and without fail they run ahead of me, or my vehicle, when they could very well fly away from me or scramble into the ditch. Is this because they are confused by what is happening? Perhaps they are unable to come up with a better plan of action on the spur of the moment.

I am reminded of the time my then-teenaged daughter decided to teach herself to ski. Using my cross-country skis, she took herself off to a steep hill on the other side of the creek, where she launched herself into space. Unfortunately for her, the dogs, ever eager for a walk, had gone with her. When they saw her turning for home they naturally did the same. At the time we had a big English Setter named Charlie, and on this occasion he proved to be "a bit of a Charlie," as they might say in England.

Jackie came swooping down the hill, with the dog right in her path. Finding herself unable to stop — she hadn't learned that bit yet — she yelled at the dog to get out of the way. Encouraged by the attention, he kept going, his long ears flapping above his head. Somehow they both managed to get to the bottom, unscathed.

I've heard a similar story that ended less happily. This was shared by a woman who dropped in to visit us some thirty years ago, hoping to see the place again. As a girl, she had come to stay with her grandparents one winter. They were settlers from Prussia who had arrived to farm this land in the 1880s. Her grandmother allowed the girl to go outside to ski, but forbade her to tackle the steep hill, which she felt was too dangerous for a beginner. Needless to say, the hill presented an exciting challenge and the child disobeyed, on the principle that what Grandma didn't know couldn't hurt her.

Like my daughter, the girl found herself unable to stop until nature took its course. She found herself in a heap on the frozen creek at the bottom of the hill, experiencing the pain of a broken leg. Nobody heard her cries for help, so the poor girl had to crawl several hundred yards uphill to the house, finally managing to reach the kitchen door, where she collapsed, exhausted.

For some reason — I think it was because a storm came up — it was three days before she could be taken to a doctor. Her grandfather did the best he could by putting horse liniment on the affected leg. Finally, she was loaded into the horse-drawn sleigh and taken out over a rough and bumpy trail through the bush, and from there over snow-packed roads to the nearest town, where there was a doctor. Country people had no telephones in those days, and the few people who had cars put them up on blocks for the winter, because there were no snowploughs either. They were hardy folk.

Years ago, it was common for children to fashion makeshift skis out of barrel staves, and I think of that when I see youngsters snowboarding, a sport which seems to have evolved from that early homemade sports equipment.

SAVE THE PLANET

A Plea from the Heart

Look thy last on all things lovely
Every hour.

In his poem "Farewell," where the above lines can be found, the English poet Walter De La Mare ponders on how the world will fare when he is dead and gone. This is a question that we might do well to ask ourselves today. As the years go by, habitats for wild creatures are shrinking, and more species are becoming threatened. Where will all this end?

Many years ago, DW encountered a great deal of criticism as a result of editorials he wrote concerning the use of pesticides on farm lands and around private homes. Part of his concern had to do with weed sprays being used on the ditches of the township roads, both in Renfrew County and farther afield. These, he suggested, could wreak havoc on the birds and small animals who made their homes there. A howl of outrage met these remarks. It seemed that just about everyone who read them thought he was a do-gooder who didn't know what he was talking about. How could farmers earn a decent living if they couldn't fight the pests that threatened their crops? How could snowplough operators do their jobs if the ditches were full of undergrowth?

Over the years, others have raised their voices in support of the environment, and, slowly, less harmful ways of dealing with these problems have been developed. The battle has not yet been won. It is only in the past few years that the citizens of some parts of Ottawa have been forbidden to spray dandelions on their lawns and green spaces. Some things are slow to change.

The more I see of the beautiful wild creatures that co-exist with me at Poison Ivy Acres, the more I'm convinced that every one of us has a responsibility to try to preserve this planet and all its inhabitants. These days it is fashionable to "go green," and this is a good start, but more is still needed by way of education.

Fortunately, much of this is available through the Renfrew County Stewardship Program, which in turn is part of Ontario Stewardship, a program of the Ontario Ministry of Natural Resources. This is a private-land conservation program that brings together landowners, organizations, and various agencies to share information and to become partners in land stewardship projects. A stewardship council directs this enterprise. Conferences, workshops, watershed projects, and a Ranger program form part of their worthwhile agenda, under which people of all ages and interests can learn and contribute. This is undoubtedly a step in the right direction, although unfortunately there is much more that needs to be done.

It seems to me that for every few people who believe in conservation, and for every one of us who loves animals and birds, there is someone else who delights in destruction. I'm not talking about farmers who shoot rogue animals in order to protect their livestock. Nor am I thinking of the culling of certain species under the direction of the Ministry of Natural Resources.

Those who kill for the joy of it are a different kettle of fish. There are those who shoot at any rare owl, hawk, or eagle they see, often because they want a mounted specimen as a trophy. There are others who shoot down heronries or Osprey's nests. There are people who bludgeon harmless snakes to death because they fear them; hunters who trespass on private land that other people try to maintain as a home for wildlife; and fishermen who poach on private ponds that have been stocked by their owners at considerable expense.

In the deer-hunting season of 2009, a bow hunter shot an innocent dog that was in its own yard, not many miles from where I live. This not only caused unnecessary suffering to the animal, but it might have injured a child of the family who might have been outside at the wrong time. It is heartwarming to note that other hunters clubbed together to raise money to help defray the dog's veterinary expenses, yet how much better it would have been if the incident had never happened. One such episode gives all responsible hunters a bad name.

Like any right-thinking person, I deplore these crimes, yet I know many people who are afraid to speak out because they fear reprisals. Even if the perpetrators are caught — and there are laws dealing with all the above misdemeanours — the fines are laughable. Those without a conscience can perpetrate their misdeeds with relative impunity.

A few years back, I was leafing through some old exercise books at a local museum. Printed inside the front covers was a directive to students, encouraging them to shoot and kill any hawks they might see, in order to protect poultry. The pigeon hawk (Merlin) and the duck hawk (Peregrine) were among those singled out. Obviously these directives were taken to heart, and the misguided information has been handed down to today's rural inhabitants, some of whom do not subscribe to current ideas. Alas, it is a long time since I've seen either of these hawks, and this alone should tell us something.

Years ago, the collecting of birds' eggs was a hobby enjoyed by many a young boy. The rarer the egg, the better the collection was thought to be. Although there are people in some parts of the world who still gloat over rare birds' eggs, I doubt if this practice is continued in our neck of the woods, and a good thing, too. The conservation of birds has a higher profile today, thanks to the growing number of naturalists' clubs and wildlife newspaper columns here in Ontario.

Climate Change

By now we must surely be aware of the problem of climate change. On one level, there doesn't seem to be a great deal that the average person can do about it and we have to trust our politicians to do the right thing on our behalf on a global level. I have to say, though, that some of the suggestions that filter down from on high only serve to emphasize the great gulf that exists between town and country.

"Plant trees!" one directive suggested. Well, I already have many thousands of them, so top marks there.

"Always try to carpool," was another bright idea, which certainly makes sense if you have to commute to work in the city but hardly works in the country. What farmer is going to wait for other like-minded neighbours to appear before going out to do the weekly grocery shopping? And machinery has to be used on the farm if food is to be produced in order to feed those city people. Nowadays, I put my car away for the winter, so, again, I'm doing my best to reduce my carbon footprint.

Why do those who supply us with electrical power keep telling us to conserve energy? I'm sure that most of us do our best, if only to keep down costs. They would do better to concentrate their efforts on big city buildings and government offices, where electric lights are kept burning all night long. What a waste that is! Supposedly this is done for security reasons, which is laughable.

I must say that I am impressed by the fact that so many country people are jumping on the green bandwagon when they can. Recycling is all the rage. Our local landfill site is one of the neatest I've seen anywhere, which is due in part to a series of watchful custodians. Top marks to them! I think, though, that rural people have always had thrifty habits. People who lived during the Great Depression or the two world wars were forced to live frugally, and recycling came naturally to them.

A great improvement has been made with the introduction of reusable shopping bags in the grocery stores. For many years now, I've used large canvas tote bags to bring my shopping home, and, having been scoffed at in the past by some people for doing this, I now feel vindicated by the stores' efforts to minimize the use of plastic.

What maddens me is the horrific amount of printed paper that ends up in my mailbox each week. Unsolicited catalogues and sample magazines, requests for money stemming from various charitable organizations, and advertising flyers from shops that we don't even have in our area. Yes, I do subscribe to a few catalogues and magazines, and I do support the charities of my choice. What I object to is the selling of subscription lists to other groups, who then flood my box with their own materials; I know who the culprits are!

I used to buy books from one well-known firm, until they started addressing me as Crol. Not only did repeated communications fail to put this right, but now I'm getting piles of junk mail under that same name. Obviously, my details have been sold to other companies. Needless to say, I no longer deal with that firm, although they continue to plague me with unsolicited offers. Other companies send me catalogues in duplicate, even in triplicate. Complaints, whether by mail, sending in the address slips, or by telephone, have no effect. The agents I speak to blame their computers, and nothing is ever done to fix the problem. Recently, steps have been taken to reduce the number of telemarketing calls that are allowed. Why can't our governments forbid the distribution of address lists?

For years now, people have been grumbling about excess packaging, yet little has changed. So many things that are offered to the consumer are covered in plastic. I try to ignore these, yet one can only go so far. I like sliced bread, but it can't be bought without a bag. So many things that have been designed for our convenience are now contributing to our downfall. Going green isn't easy. It takes time and energy.

As I look around, rejoicing in the natural world around me while believing that "Man" is his own worst enemy, I realize that the clergyman and hymn writer Reverend Reginald Heber (1783–1823) hit the nail on the head with his words: "Every prospect pleases, but only man is vile."

Please, won't you commit to doing your part to saving our planet and the wildlife that shares it with us? It all depends on you.

PART III:
BIRD TALES

THE MAGIC TREE

Outside my office window, there is what I think of as a magic tree; it certainly lives up to its nickname. It is an Amur Maple (*Acer ginnala*), a native of Japan. Twenty-five years ago, we planted two such trees at some distance from the house, and since then clones have been springing up all over the place, growing rapidly. Annoyingly, when I have scattered seeds in places where I'd like to see more of these trees growing, and even when I have buried some, nothing happens. Wild creatures beat me to it.

Some gardening books describe this maple as a delicate shrub that must be handled gently, but this doesn't seem to be the case with the magic tree. Branches expand by several feet in length each year, and I occasionally have to lop one off when a high wind brings it too close to the window, threatening the glass. Some branches are scarred where woodpeckers have been at work, and other have broken off during snowstorms, but still the tree seems indestructible.

This particular tree stands a few feet away from my kitchen window, and its upper branches reach past the window of my upstairs office. There is something to recommend it at every season of the year. Its green flowers attract bees in spring. In summer, its leaves provide shade for resting birds. In autumn, its foliage is a glorious backdrop to my work, when chipmunks work industriously to gather the crimson keys. Snow and ice make the tree a thing of beauty in winter.

The roof of the one-storey laundry room is sheltered by its branches, and in winter this makes a handy bird feeder when I throw seeds out my office window. Squirrels use the tree as a means of access, and at times a tap on the glass causes me to look up to see a raccoon peering in. If I open the window and hold out a piece of bread, the animal accepts it in its long black fingers.

On a typical day in winter, the resident birds land on the tree before hopping down to the roof. Blue Jays, Black-capped Chickadees, White-breasted and Red-breasted Nuthatches, Tree Sparrows and Evening Grosbeaks, and sometimes Goldfinches, Purple Finches, Redpolls, and the occasional Hoary Redpoll. Hairy and Downy Woodpeckers enjoy sunflower seeds, and they eat these by lying flat on their bellies on the sloping roof, which is an amusing sight.

Summer and fall visitors perch briefly in this tree, including various flycatchers, vireos, and warblers. I catch a glimpse of these while working at the computer, and although I keep binoculars to hand, they are seldom needed because the birds are so close to the window. In

Working peacefully together, a Black-capped Chickadee and a Downy Woodpecker enjoy an offering of suet.

this way I can observe birds that I might not see in the field, such as the tiny Ruby-crowned or Golden-crowned Kinglet.

I do a lot of birdwatching while working at the kitchen sink. In autumn, a variety of thrushes forage among the fallen leaves at the base of the magic tree, searching for insects and other delicacies. In a typical year, I might see one of the following, although not, of course, all at the same time: Grey-cheeked Thrush, Swainson's Thrush, Hermit Thrush, and Wood Thrush. Another small thrush, the Veery, comes early in the spring and can be found throughout Poison Ivy Acres.

When I report an uncommon sighting to the bird columnist at our weekly newspaper, readers sometimes remark that I must spend hours searching out these birds. This isn't true. I'm sure that I'd see even more birds if I spent hours each day rambling around the property, but I have other things to do. These sightings are a reward for doing the dishes or getting busy at the computer, and they are all a result of having the Amur Maple growing there.

It truly is a magic tree, and I would advise any birdwatcher to plant one near the house. You will be rewarded many times over.

STRICTLY FOR THE BIRDS

"Come quickly! There's a slate-covered junkie outside my door!" The lady's excitement transmitted itself over our rural telephone line. I was glad that she couldn't see me grinning.

For some years, I wrote a bird column in what was then my local weekly newspaper. In this, I described the birds that were seen in our district from time to time. The column was popular with readers because I always mentioned by name the people who had seen something interesting, and they vied with each other to turn in some interesting reports.

Some of the readers were keen birders, who went out on weekends, armed with field guides and binoculars. They could always be relied on to turn out for the annual Christmas Audubon Bird Count. These were the folk who could identify specimens at a glance, and could be relied upon to give a correct account of what they had seen.

Others were not as expert, although just as keen to join in the fun. They would phone up in the hope of getting their sightings verified. Various routine questions were asked as we strove to arrive at a positive identification.

How big was the bird — robin-sized, or as large as a crow? Wing bars, or no wing bars? Could they describe the shape of the tail, the colour of the legs, the type of beak? What was it doing when it was seen?

There was always great excitement when some rare visitor arrived. Here the rule of thumb was that no positive claim could be made without witnesses. That is, the sighting had to have been observed and verified by more than one person.

The lady who phoned had seen a Northern Junco, which at that time was known as a Slate-coloured Junco (*Junco hyemalis*). The previous week, I had described this bird, explaining that flocks of them had just arrived back in the area. The juncos are sparrow-like birds, slate grey in colour, with white outer tail feathers. In fact, they often travel in flocks with certain sparrows. They come to our part of Canada twice a year, in the spring and fall, travelling between their northern summer habitat and Mexico and the southern United States, where they spend the winter. They spend a month or so here each time, and their coming heralds the changing seasons.

A fairly common summer visitor to Poison Ivy Acres is the Brown Thrasher (*Toxostoma rufum*). A member of the Family *Mimidae*, the thrasher, along with the Catbird and the Mockingbird, is sometimes referred to as a mimic thrush. While it resembles some of the thrushes in appearance, it is quite a bit larger than they are, and it has wing bars, which they do not. The thrasher's upper body is a bright rufous colour, and it is heavily striped below. This handsome bird has a long tail, a curved bill, and yellow eyes.

Long before I came to Poison Ivy Acres, I had described such a bird for our readers, to give them something of interest to look out for, having just spotted one myself. The following week I had just stepped outside the newspaper office when a man hailed me from across the street.

"Hey there! I seen one of them brown flashers you wrote about last week."

Thanking him for his interest, I didn't have the heart to tell him that what he'd actually seen was a thrasher. Besides, a passing lady had stopped nearby, as if turned to stone, and was listening to us with her mouth open. Obviously she was not a faithful follower of my column.

 ## WATCHING THE BIRDS

If birdwatchers sometimes make me laugh, so do the birds themselves. I know it's silly to think of them as having human attributes, but sometimes they behave just like us!

One of the prettiest summer visitors to Poison Ivy Acres is the Baltimore or Northern Oriole (*Icterus galbula*). The male bird is a brilliant orange colour with a black head, while his mate is olive-brown above and yellowish below. They have white wing bars. Orioles have a very sweet song, a sort of piping whistle.

When I was a young Girl Guide in Wales, we used to sing a song that had probably come from the United States:

Come to the woods with carefree song
To hear the golden oriole.
For if that minstrel you should hear
Know that summer must be near.

There are several species of oriole in the United States, so I don't know which one the song-writer had in mind. The Baltimore Oriole builds a pouch-like nest, which is suspended from the branch of a tall tree. In these nests the young are nurtured in a sort of rocking cradle. The orioles' tree of choice used to be the White Elm, but the Dutch Elm disease robbed them of their favourite nesting places. In more recent years at our home, they have chosen Manitoba Maples instead.

One spring I watched, fascinated, while a male oriole did his best to weave such a nest, while his spouse sat on a nearby fence and watched him. Alas, the result was a very lopsided affair that would have blown apart at the first gust of wind. Was this his first attempt at nest building? It did seem as if DIY was not his thing. His mate began to squawk. She flew up to inspect the nest and came back down to the fence, obviously dis-gruntled. The male flew back up and had another go, but the result was no better. He returned, and perched on the fence beside her.

An Eastern Bluebird atop its summer home. Before flying south, these birds come back to inspect the nesting boxes, as if choosing a site to return to the following year.

Suddenly, it seemed as if she could stand it no longer. She got up and gave him a few whacks with her wing, then jabbed at him with her beak. I had just seen a real live hen-pecked husband! It occurs to me now that this expression may have come about after some long-ago birdwatcher observed birds in action.

A female Hairy Woodpecker (*Picoides villosus*) was more self-reliant when it came to finding a place to raise a family. Woodpeckers are cavity nesters, but for some reason she didn't seem to feel like boring a hole in a tree, despite the fact that she was living in the middle of a wood. No, what she fancied was a proper house with a roof. She inspected all the man-made bluebird boxes and finally settled on the one of her choice, but there was a problem. She couldn't get inside. The entrance hole of a bluebird box is deliberately made small, to keep out predators and larger nesting birds. This woodpecker set to work to enlarge the hole, which was no problem with her strong beak.

What I found amusing was the way in which she stopped every few minutes to test out her handiwork. She tried to get through the hole by wriggling violently, like a woman trying to get into a too-small corset. The bird then had to back out and begin again. Although she was making the box useless for the needs of nesting bluebirds, I didn't have the heart to chase such an enterprising bird away.

Another enterprising bird was the Barn Swallow that built her nest above my office window. I enjoyed watching the little family as they grew. Eventually the mother chose each youngster in turn to take a flying lesson. When it came to the last and smallest one, it refused to leave the nest, teetering on the edge. At last, losing patience, his parent gave him a wallop with her wing, and off he went, luckily getting the hang of things before he reached the ground.

 ## WHERE VULTURES DANCE

What would your reaction be if a flock of giant birds landed on your roof? No, I'm not fantasizing about a group of storks, heralding the birth of twins!

My home is back in the bush, with no neighbours close by, and because it's so quiet it's a great spot for birdwatching. Spring is an exciting time, when visitors of the feathered variety arrive and mate. It never ceases to amaze me that, after a flight of perhaps thousands of miles, certain birds will find their way back to the very same nesting site that they have used before.

One day in early April, I was working away at my computer when I happened to glance out of the window to see a Turkey Vulture crouching on top of the sugar shack. This in itself was unusual; vultures are normally seen on the ground, feeding, or floating unsteadily around the sky, soaring in wide circles. I wondered if the bird had just come down to rest, exhausted after its long flight north.

However, the next time I looked up the bird had moved to the high-peaked roof of our guest house, where it was soon joined by three more vultures. This log building, which is long and very tall, was converted from a former horse stable, cow byre, and second-storey hayloft. The birds seemed to be staring at the house, and I wondered why. This was beginning to feel like a Hitchcock movie!

The former cow byre and horse stable. The vultures' courtship ritual took place on this peaked roof, and the Whip-poor-will likes to roost above the door.

Turkey Vultures (*Cathartes aura*) are summer visitors to our part of Canada, and very useful they are, too, being carrion eaters. They clean up the remains of animals killed on the roads. Unfortunately, many people despise them because they are rather ugly with their small, bald, red heads. But, to the true birdwatcher, anything that flies is worth observing.

I longed to grab my camera to get photos of this sight, but I was afraid I'd scare them off if I opened a door or window, so I decided instead to watch from behind the curtains to see what happened next. To my amazement, I was about to witness something that is seldom seen by birdwatchers here: the courtship ritual of the Turkey Vulture. In fact, this is such a rare sighting that the birding experts I later spoke to weren't sure what the usual procedure is, suggesting that possibly the event takes place on the ground.

All four vultures were sitting in a row on the peaked roof. I was reminded of a line from a game we used to play when my children were small: "Two little birdies, sitting on a wall, one named Peter, the other named Paul...."

Male and female vultures look alike, so at first I couldn't tell their gender until the first bird stood up and began to dance. Turkey Vultures have a six-foot wingspan, so when this bird spread his wings to their fullest extent, straight out from the shoulder, it was an awe-inspiring sight. He began to stamp his feet while dancing in ever-increasing circles, which was no easy feat on the narrow roof peak. I once saw a documentary in which a Native American performed an eagle dance, his outstretched arms covered in feathers. The behaviour of this vulture was much the same, except that it was dancing on large red feet instead of moccasins.

The other three birds stared glumly ahead until finally one of them took notice. She favoured him with an occasional glance, quickly followed by a pointed stare in the opposite direction. Her suitor was forced to dance even harder to get her attention. (Vultures seldom make any sound, so he was unable to shout the avian version of "look at me!")

When she decided he'd suffered enough, she flew off her perch and he followed. Soon the pair were swooping and diving all over the sky, in what seemed to be an exhibition of joy. Meanwhile, the other two birds stayed on the roof, motionless for a long time. I could only assume that they were not another breeding pair; perhaps they were two of the same gender. The mating pair flew in circles for hours. Eventually the other birds left the roof and disappeared.

I have wondered since if my two birds raised their young on my property. This might not be so, because vultures range over a wide territory. Still, my land, with its rocky terrain, is ideal for them. Turkey Vultures don't built nests. They lay their eggs — usually two — in a protected site such as a rock crevice in thick cover.

Some bird books state that the vulture's breeding range in this northern part of its territory is poorly known, but we have been seeing them in our area for forty years or more. Although this is the first time I've been privileged to see their courtship ritual, I think they may have attempted to raise their young here in the past. Some years ago I found a very large speckled egg on a rock beneath some juniper bushes. I feel sure that it belonged to a Turkey Vulture. When the young vulture hatches, it is cared for by both parents, who regurgitate carrion for the fledgling. The youngster will be ready to fly when it reaches the age of eleven weeks.

I enjoy watching young birds learning to fly. I have seen a Cooper's Hawk apparently demonstrating technique to a juvenile. This is a leisurely activity because these hawks live on my property year-round. By contrast, the young vulture has to learn this skill quickly because these birds leave our area in mid-October to head south for the winter. Presumably the juvenile begins by learning to flex its wings, just like dad during the courtship ritual. I just wish I could be there to see it. Who knows? Perhaps someday, I shall.

THE GIANT NEST

Thirty years ago, DW helped build a giant nest, and it is still in use today. Here's how it happened.

Being always on the go, he spent much of his time with a chainsaw in his hand. There was firewood to be cut for winter use, often with the help of one of his friends. The wood was brought home on a sleigh drawn by a snowmobile. After that, my job was to operate the wood splitter, and then stack the logs in the woodshed.

As well as this, there were nine miles of hiking trails to be kept open. Branches that were too sparse for firewood went to make brush piles, which in turn would provide shelter for birds and small woodland creatures.

One spring day, DW was working away on the other side of the creek, lopping branches from some young Red Pines beside a trail. His method was to leave the good-sized branches lying where they were, with the intention of returning the next day to make them into a new brush pile. A Red-tailed Hawk (*Buteo jamaicensis*) had other ideas. The bird had selected another nearby pine tree in which to make a nest. This tree is perhaps seventy or eighty feet tall. We watched from the house in amazement as the hawk picked up the weighty fallen branches and carried them up into the tree. It began to build a nest near the trunk on a huge jutting branch, far above the ground.

Harrison's *Field Guide to Nests, Eggs and Nestlings of North American Birds* states that the nest of the Red-tailed Hawk is a bulky structure of twigs, but in this case the bird had chosen the freshly cut boughs, which in some cases were as thick as my wrist. It built its home to last, and the nest is in use to this day, although not always inhabited by hawks!

In due course, a small family was raised, and, when autumn came, off they flew to winter in Panama or somewhere equally far from home. We looked forward to seeing them again in the spring. Would they return to the same spot?

The answer is that yes, they did return, but not to nest in the big pine tree. A pair of Great Horned Owls (*Bubo virginianus*) had beaten them to it. The hawks stayed at Poison Ivy Acres until they left again in the fall, but we never did discover where they nested.

After that, it was a toss-up who got to the nest first. There was no rhyme or reason to this. The first Red-tailed Hawk always returns in March, usually on St. Patrick's Day, unless there happens to be a snowstorm. It flies a few circuits over the sugar shack, as if to say "Hello! Look at me, I'm back."

On the other hand, the owls are here all year round. They can be heard calling to each other in February. The female fires off a volley of up to eight hoots; the male responds with fewer. It is a mystery to me why these owls take up residence in the old pine tree in certain years, while in others they leave it vacant for the coming of the hawks.

Is there some strange phenomenon at work here, known only to birds? I have seen bluebirds checking out nesting boxes before they leave in the fall, probably deciding to return to that same spot in the spring. Is it possible that hawks can put a mark on their nest, signalling their intention to return there in six month's time? This sounds fanciful, yet there are many things we don't understand about bird behaviour. I can only marvel at the fact that a bird of any sort is capable of flying thousands of miles back to Poison Ivy Acres, to return to the very same nest it used the year before. This seems to me to be a miracle in itself.

 ## THE DANCING GROUSE

Coming home from town one spring day I saw an amazing sight. A Ruffed Grouse (*Bonasa umbellus*) was performing its courtship dance in the middle of my narrow lane, while a

second bird, presumably female, wandered nearby, pretending not to notice. The male was so absorbed in what it was doing that it didn't seem to realize I was there, and I had to stop the car so as not to run him down.

This bird derives its name from the black "ruffs" on the side of its neck. These are features that are not always easy to spot in the field. Now, while the grouse was performing for its mate, dark feathers on his head were falling over its face like a long black wig. As the bird strutted, I was disappointed not to see its tail displayed in a colourful fan, as shown in the

A Ruffed Grouse stands near her nest, which is well-hidden from possible predators. Grouse usually select a nesting site beneath an evergreen tree.

bird books, but probably this phase had occurred earlier, when he was first trying to attract a female. I had heard the male birds drumming some weeks before. This sound, which is referred to as "the drumming of the partridge," is made by rapidly beating the wings.

I should explain that this bird is referred to locally as a partridge, although grouse and partridge are actually two different species. The Ruffed Grouse nests on the ground, more often than not at the base of a spruce tree. I have observed that grouse seldom venture far from the place where they were hatched, and when I'm searching for some of them (at the time of the Christmas Bird Count, for example) I usually find them close to a spruce or cedar tree.

A shallow depression is scraped out and lined with soft material, such as dead leaves and fallen pine or spruce needles, and as many as a dozen eggs are laid. These, cream-coloured or beige, are about the size of a pullet's egg. At one time, I often used to see female grouse out walking, followed by a large number of young, but no more. There are too many predators about, including raccoons and crows, which will steal the eggs, as well as larger creatures that prey on the juveniles. Having a large brood is nature's way of ensuring the survival of the species.

Nowadays, I seldom see more than half a dozen chicks at a time, and in the summer of 2009, I was saddened to see a female grouse herding a single youngster down the lane. I am beginning to wonder if there are other factors to blame for this decline. It seems to me that adult grouse have few means of protecting their young, other than the well-known practice of drawing off predators with the broken-wing act. I have on occasion come up behind a grouse family on the lane, both of us being out for a walk, and the adult bird has responded by running ahead of me, as fast as her legs will carry her, leaving her brood to straggle on behind. Eventually, the young ones peel off into the verges until the mother follows suit. Whether this is a calculated move on her part, or a confused retreat, I can't say. Whatever it is, the birds are in no danger from me, nor do they pose any threat to me in return.

 ## BANDIT BIRDS

Little masked bandits. That's how I think of the birds with black eye masks that I've seen. The shrikes really are predators, depending on small birds, mice, and insects for their food. There are two species in North America, members of the Family *Laniidae*, both of which visit Poison Ivy Acres, although at different times of year.

They are the Northern Shrike (*Lanius excubitor*) and the Loggerhead Shrike (*Lanius ludovicianus*). In addition to their distinctive eye masks, shrikes are recognizable by their black wings with a white patch. The mask of the Northern Shrike ends at the bill, while that of the Loggerhead extends over the bill.

Shrikes have hook-tipped bills that enable them to tear their prey apart. They behave rather like hawks, perching on wires or treetops, waiting to swoop down when something suitable comes into view. One day in late autumn, I saw two shrikes working together, a sight that one seldom sees because, like the hawks, they are solitary hunters. Walking up the hill behind the barn I saw, out of the corner of my eye, a shrike perched in a young elm. A closer look revealed an immature bird on another branch. The juvenile is brown, but of course it has the distinctive hooked bill, so it's not hard to identify.

As I watched, the shrike swooped down on some unfortunate creature on the ground and, after a moment's hesitation, the youngster followed. I wasn't sure what I was seeing, because I don't know how long the juveniles remain with their parent. I wondered if perhaps this one was being taught how to hunt. Pleased with what I had seen, I turned and walked away.

Waxwings are also masked birds, but the only living things they hunt down are insects, although they prefer berries. These are the Bohemian Waxwing (*Bombycilla garrulous*) and the Cedar Waxwing (*Bombycilla cedrorum*). These beautiful birds resemble each other with their crested heads, eye masks, and yellow-tipped tails. Unlike the Cedar Waxwing, the Bohemian Waxwing has reddish under-tail coverts, hard to spot in the field. The two species arrive at different times of year, preferring bright red berries when they can find them.

At my place, they enjoy the fruit of the honeysuckle shrubs, but a friend usually has an invasion of waxwings when her Rowan berries are at their best. When all else fails, they will resort to juniper berries. I'll never forget the time I went walking down to the beaver meadow, where I flushed up an enormous cloud of these colourful birds that were working away on the prickly bushes.

The smallest of Poison Ivy's bandit birds, but with the most distinctive eye mask of all, is the male Common Yellowthroat (*Geothlypsis trichas*). This is a wood warbler, which often visits Poison Ivy Acres in summer. It's always a red-letter day when this bird, with its black mask and bright yellow throat, lands in the Amur Maple. Being an insect eater, it usually has a wide choice of food, and seemingly is unafraid of the Eastern Phoebes picking off flies close by.

THE GROUND NESTERS

Often, when taking visitors for a walk around Poison Ivy Acres, I notice an astonishing fact. Many people look straight ahead, or at me, chattering as they go. They don't look up, unless some loud bird call attracts them, and they seldom look down, unless they are trying to negotiate a tricky bit of swampland.

Of course this doesn't apply to field naturalists, amateur or otherwise, all of whom are eager to observe everything that the countryside has to offer. It is the full-time city people who fail to open their eyes to the natural world around them. Perhaps they are so used to ignoring the noise and bustle of their usual habitat that their appreciation of what nature has to offer has been blunted.

"I love the country," one lady told me, as we strolled along. "You know, I never miss watching a nature program when they have one on television."

It's too bad that she allows herself to ignore the real thing. We were crossing the hidden field, a large expanse surrounded by maple trees, which at that time were in all their glorious fall array. "Just look at that!" I enthused, with a wave of my hand.

"Mmm," she replied, lifting her head for a moment. Then, she went on with her account of what one colleague had said to another, and didn't I think it was a disgrace?

Each spring, I spend a lot of time looking down at the ground. Some birds build their nests there, while others do not make nests at all, laying their eggs in depressions lined with leaf material. The Ruffed Grouse (*Bonasa umbellus*), Wilson's Snipe (*Capella gallinago*), Upland Sandpiper (*Bartramia longicauda*), and the Woodcock (*Philohela minor*) are among the latter that habitually raise families at Poison Ivy Acres. In one never-to-be-forgotten year, a Marsh Hawk or Northern Harrier (*Circus cyaneus*) made its nest in the middle of the hayfield, which seemed like a risky place to be, although the adult birds are certainly strong enough to deal with predators. The hawk will fly away, in an attempt to lure unwelcome visitors away. Bobolinks (*Dolichonyx oryzivorus*) also favour that field, laying eggs in a little grass cup.

Over the years, I have located the nesting sites of all these birds, usually by accident, but so far I have failed to find the nest of the Ovenbird (*Seiurus aurocapillus*). It is a common enough bird here, and I always know when they have returned in the spring because of their characteristic call of "teacher, teacher, teacher."

The bird derives its name from the shape of its nest, which resembles a dutch oven.

According to the bird books, this is a domed structure that is well-camouflaged with leaves and forest-floor debris. It has a side entrance that is invisible from above. Once, when climbing up to the edge of the hardwood bush, I flushed an Ovenbird out of the ground, and I was careful to take note of the exact spot where it had erupted, which happened to be close to my feet. I was about to see an Ovenbird's nest!

I shuffled forward as carefully as possible, not wanting to inflict damage. I squatted down, the better to see what I was looking for, but the nest was too well-hidden. Disappointed, I backed away. I knew I might have uncovered the nest by sweeping the vegetation aside with my feet, but I wasn't there to cause harm. I believe that when we choose to live in harmony with wild things they should be treated with respect. In retrospect I know I should have marked the spot and returned in the fall to hunt for the nest when the birds had flown.

The Eastern Meadowlark (*Sturnella magna*) is another bird that constructs a dome-shaped nest. I have never come across one, although this bird, with its distinctive yellow breast sporting a black

The nest of the Ruffed Grouse, with ten pale buff-coloured eggs.

An American Woodcock watches warily as DW approaches her nest, camera in hand. Earthworms are the woodcock's food of choice.

tie, is often seen in the hayfields in spring. *Perhaps this year?* I ask myself. The great thing about country life is that there is always something to look forward to.

AN EXPLOSION!

There is nothing like a peaceful ramble through the winter woods, wearing snowshoes. All sound is deadened by a new fall of snow, and nature seems to be asleep, waiting for the return of spring. Such an outing is good for the soul, all the stresses of daily life left far in the background.

That is what I thought, until a violent explosion occurred. I can't say who was the more alarmed — me, or the startled grouse that burst out of the snowbank right in front of me with a flurry of wings. As I stood there, trying to slow my pounding heart rate, I realized that I had witnessed a phenomenon I'd read about, but never seen. When a storm is threatened, a Ruffed Grouse will burrow into a snowbank and stay there until the weather improves.

I had inadvertently trodden on the poor creature, although I don't think it could have been hurt. My weight was evenly distributed because I wearing Algonquin snowshoes. Still, the sleeping bird must have been jerked into wakefulness, with its fight or flight mechanism fully activated.

Most of the time, grouse like to stay close to the earth. They nest on the ground, and they like to walk about in their search for food. In winter I often see their tracks as they wander back and forth across the lane. That is not to say that they won't fly when they want to. I have learned to be wary when walking beneath cedars or spruce trees. A disturbed grouse will fly out of the tree with great violence, its flight path horizontal rather than vertical. I have a nasty feeling that if we ever made contact it could almost take my head off, or at least do serious damage. One would not think that this timid, rather stupid bird could cause such grief, but such is indeed the case. On several occasions I have found a grouse near the house with a broken neck, caused by a collision with window glass. This bird has a powerful flight indeed.

The Ruffed Grouse (*Bonasa umbellus*) occurs in two colour morphs. Grey tails are seen in the birds' grey phase, and red in the red phase. According to Peterson's *Field Guide to the Birds*, "Red birds are in preponderance in the southern parts of the range, gray birds northward." I have seen both types at Poison Ivy Acres, although it isn't always easy to spot the difference when the bird is flushed from the ground, disappearing swiftly in a whirr of wings.

However, I frequently meet these birds on the lane when both of us are on foot, and then the grouse runs ahead of me, going faster and faster, occasionally giving a little hop off the ground. Eventually it veers off into the undergrowth, having given me a good view of its back and tail. Why grouse don't melt into the weeds immediately is something of a mystery, because their camouflage is excellent. Unless they are alarmed, as in the case of my snowbank experience, they don't seem to have much sense of self-preservation. As a result, many of them fall prey to hunters in the fall.

THE BARKING TURKEY

One morning in December, thirteen Wild Turkeys arrived at my feeders, pecking at sunflower seeds that had fallen to the ground. The chickadees, redpolls, and Tree Sparrows didn't seem at all intimidated by these enormous birds, which don't seem to be aggressive in any way to either man or beast. Wild Turkeys were introduced into our area several years ago, and these were part of a flock of some two dozen turkeys that were hatched at Poison Ivy Acres the previous spring.

About an hour after my visitors had moved on from the feeders, I went out to collect the mail. All the way to my mailbox, which is a mile away from the house, I followed the flock's tracks in the snow, noting the erratic progress they'd made as they searched for food during their trek. On returning home, I decided to bring in some firewood while I still had my boots on. The woodshed is some distance away from the house, and when I reached it, I could hear loud, anguished barking coming from somewhere nearby. I assumed I was hearing a dog — a very large dog that most probably had been lost in the bush by hunters back in the November deer-hunting season. It wouldn't be the first time that a missing dog had arrived at my door early in the winter, hungry and exhausted.

I could hardly believe it when I discovered that the noise was coming from a hen turkey! She had apparently walked through the open gate of the nearby dog pen and she didn't have the sense to leave by the same route. She kept jabbing her beak through the chain-link fence in a desperate attempt to break free.

She was so alarmed when she saw me coming to help that she flew up into the air, clearing the seven-foot fence by at least a yard. Who would have thought that such a bulky bird could take off vertically to reach such a height? I was just thankful that she hadn't flown sideways, as startled grouse often do, or I could have been badly injured. I know of more than one person whose car windshield has been shattered after a collision with a turkey. The last I saw of her, she was scuttling up the lane in the direction her chums had taken.

I have since been told by a birding expert that barking is indeed one of the sounds that Wild Turkeys are known to make. However, he hasn't experienced this phenomenon himself, and neither have other birders I've spoken to, so I feel privileged indeed to have witnessed this behaviour.

Sometimes I meet up with these turkeys when I'm out walking. In the spring, it's delightful to see the young ones, not much bigger than a robin. It's amazing to see how quickly the poults grow to their full size. Quite often one of the adult males bars my way until his harem is safely off the trail, but I have never heard them make a sound. This is why what happened to me on this occasion was such a surprise.

Wild Turkeys (*Meleagris gallopavo*) are handsome birds, especially when the male fans out his tail in a courtship display. The male is polygamous, having several mates that share a nesting site on the ground, staying together to protect the hatchlings. At Poison Ivy Acres, they usually choose to settle down in the vegetation at the edge of one of my hayfields.

Bird books say that the hen lays ten to fifteen eggs, which means that if there are several hens at the same site, there should be a large number of poults as a result. However, the most I have seen out walking, accompanied by a male and three females, is a total of fifteen juveniles. Crows can sometimes be heard cawing triumphantly as they leave the site, which probably means that they have feasted on the eggs or hatchlings. Skunks and raccoons also eat birds' eggs when they find them.

I have noticed that from early fall onwards these families range over a wide area, mostly on foot, although they will fly for short distances. They feed on berries, seeds, and insects, and often, when I see them pecking their way along the township road, I wonder how their meagre findings can possibly sustain such large bodies.

Despite their large size, Wild Turkeys are swift runners, picking up their feet much as geese will do. Sometimes, coming over the hill near my gate, when driving home from town, I have to brake suddenly when I find the road full of turkeys. Instead of veering off to the side, they run ahead of the car, moving faster and faster, sometimes giving little hops off the ground. A light beep of the horn sends them flying up into the trees, and then I can drive on.

While walking up the lane at twilight, I once inadvertently flushed a turkey out of a cedar tree, where it had been roosting. I don't know which of us was the more startled, but the bird flew across the field and into the bush, obviously wanting to put as much distance between us as possible. I'd never seen a Wild Turkey fly so far before. Usually they seem content to wander across the ground, within a mile or two of their nesting sites.

CAT CALLS

With a mew mew here and a mew mew there
Here a mew, there a mew, everywhere a mew mew,
ee-eye, ee-eye- o!

As Poison Ivy Acres has several house cats, it should come as no surprise to anyone that the air is frequently rent with cat language. My alarm clock no sooner goes off in the morning than Rufus is pounding up the stairs, wailing mournfully outside the bedroom door. Despite the fact that the bowl of kibble in the kitchen has probably been emptied overnight, he wants to let me know that he is in imminent danger of starvation, a suggestion belied by his portly figure.

His roommate, Ruby, is content to wait quietly, although as soon as I appear a display of cupboard love begins, as she rubs against my legs, purring loudly. On occasion, Ruby gives vent to a series of low growls, usually when a marauding squirrel appears on the windowsill. If a strange cat dares approach the house, Ruby wails and shrieks. If I had ever thought of keeping such a thing as a kitty-swear box, it would be filled up quickly!

Strangely, when various other mews are heard outside, she minds her own business. These sounds are made by visiting birds, and Ruby knows the difference. She may greet the sounds with a useless lashing of her tail, but that is as far as it goes. Two of these birds, which come close to the house, are the Gray Catbird (*Dumetella carolinenis*), which belongs to the Family *Mimidae* ("mimic thrushes") and the Yellow-bellied Sapsucker (*Sphyrapicus varius*), of the Family *Picidae*. Both make cat-like sounds.

The catbird is a slate-grey bird, slightly smaller than a robin, with a black cap. When perching, it flips its tail. It usually nests near the house and can often be seen flitting through the lilacs, although I've never found its nest there. It often sits in the nearby spruce, uttering its plaintive mew. Unfortunately this coniferous tree is so dense that, even in winter, any possible nests remain invisible.

The sapsucker, a handsome woodpecker, also stays near the house, and in the fall a single immature bird usually comes to the Amur Maple. It has a nasal mew, which, if anything, is more feline-sounding than the catbird. Several trees near the house, especially a flowering crabapple, which has dark red blossoms in spring, are favourites of the sapsuckers, who drill orderly rows of holes in the bark to get at the sap. Needless to say, this isn't good for the tree, and, if I had to choose, I can't make up my mind which I'd prefer to see in future years, the handsome bird or the glorious display of blossoms. Needless to say, the sapsucker takes the decision out of my hands.

These two birds are common visitors to Poison Ivy Acres, but one warm night in the fall we heard a quite different bird making a loud mewing whine. The bedroom windows were open, and I was sure that a stray cat was outside, so I looked to Ruby for confirmation. She wasn't interested. The sounds seemed to be coming from the spruce tree outside the window. Still not convinced that it wasn't a cat, I switched on an outside light, but that was a waste of time, as whatever it was must have been close to the trunk rather than sitting on the outer branches. Turning off the light, I went back upstairs.

Now the sound was coming from another tree, and over the course of the next hour it seemed to originate in a number of places. Obviously, this was a bird, but I had never heard anything like it before. What could it be? Having consulted my field guide, I decided that it might be a Long-eared Owl (*Asio otus*). Reaching for our tapes of bird calls, I played the appropriate segment, and bingo! Our evening visitor responded with a long drawn-out hoot. Another feathered addition to my life list!

A MALLARD AT BAY

Is it my imagination, or are crows becoming more numerous and more aggressive these days? In the spring they seem to hunt in packs, and it's a common sight to see some poor little bird valiantly trying to drive these big, black birds away from her nest. It's bad enough when I find broken eggshells on the ground, but when I see a crow carrying off a struggling fledgling, it's almost too much to bear. After all, the Common Crow is designed by nature to eat almost anything, so it does seem particularly unfair when more attractive little birds, such as robins, have their nests robbed by these predators.

I enjoy watching ducks, and the Mallard (*Anas platyrhynchos*) is always one of the first to come to Poison Ivy Acres in the spring. It seems that they choose their mates before arriving, for when they land in the pond there are usually two of them. The male is easily recognizable, with his glossy green head and bright yellow bill. He has a chestnut-coloured chest, and the rest of his body is mainly grey, with a blue patch or speculum at the base of the wing. The female is a mottled brown colour, similar to other marsh ducks. This is nature's camouflage, intended to keep the bird safe from predators, because mallards nest on the ground. Alas, this is not always sufficient to protect them from the crows.

I heard them coming one morning, their loud clamour alerting others of their kind. I looked out to see the sky over the pond black with approaching birds. It reminded me of Daphne Du Maurier's story, "The Birds," which was adapted into a movie by Alfred Hitchcock.

I had suspected that the Mallard had a nest hidden in the tall grass on the bank, and, sure enough, she rose into the air and flew a little distance away. Whether this was the typical broken-wing act, or simply that that she feared for her own safety, I couldn't say, but I was infuriated on her behalf. Grabbing a broom, I raced down the hill, shouting and waving my weapon. So might Boadicea have faced the Roman hordes. I had once chased a Charolais bull out of the corn patch with that same broom, so I knew that some creatures regarded it as a fearsome thing.

A Mallard rises from her nest beside the pond near the house.

I had arrived in time. The nest seemed undisturbed. The eggs were covered with a dear little blanket to keep them warm; the duck pulls down from its breast for this purpose. Not wanting to leave my scent on the nest, I didn't peep inside to see how many eggs there were, but I know that Mallards usually lay about a dozen or so. After a few more forays, the crows seemed to give up the idea and retreated to look for a nest that didn't have a mad woman on guard beside it. I hoped that the fledglings survived. They usually take to water soon after hatching, so it may be that the mother duck took them down to the creek in due course.

On another occasion, I had an encounter with crows that surprised me. When cleaning out the fridge, I removed several eggs that were well past their sell-by date. These, I thought, would please the raccoons. They are always partial to a nice egg, which they will carefully break open and eat. I had no sooner put the eggs out on the lawn when several

A pair of Mallards enjoy life at the pond on a spring morning.

167

crows swooped down and appropriated them. Where had they come from so suddenly, and how did that know that the eggs were there? Why did they fancy eggs that were cold from the fridge and smelling of humankind?

Nature guards so many little mysteries like this, and trying to understand them is one of the pleasures of living in the country.

BLUE AND THE MERGANSER

Blue was a cheerful and gentle English Setter of the Blue Belton variety. With several champions in his lineage, he was registered under the name Nirvanas Juniper Blue. His brother, an Orange Belton, was Nirvanas Juniper Jordan, known as Jordie. The juniper is the plant badge of the Clan MacLeod of Harris, of which the McCuaigs are a sept, and since Poison Ivy Acres is overrun by juniper bushes, the name seemed apt.

These dogs were bought as companion animals and were not destined for the show ring. Nor were they trained as field dogs, although setters are bred for that. Our dogs led a life that included several long walks each day, no matter what the season. What more could any dog ask for?

Blue had the thick fur common to Blue Beltons, as opposed to the silky fur coat that nature had bestowed on his brother. He loved to swim, and, whenever possible in winter, he would plunge through the ice into the creek, and come out grinning in delight. One summer day, he went into that same creek and came back carrying a young Hooded Merganser (*Lophodytes cucullatus*), which he laid at his master's feet, a look of devotion on his doggy face. I doubt that he understood why he received such a scolding. He watched dejectedly as DW carefully returned the bird to its mother's keeping. There is nothing to equal the look on a setter's face to make his owner feel guilty! Then, we herded the four dogs along, so that there was no chance of the incident being repeated.

As it happened, no harm was done. Setters have lovely soft mouths, and Blue had been gentle. When he had dived into the water, the female merganser and her numerous offspring had scattered in all directions, and although she gave some indignant squawks at the disturbance, it didn't seem as though she had missed one of her brood.

Each year the Hooded Mergansers are among the first spring birds to return to Poison Ivy Acres, sometimes followed by a pair of Common Mergansers (*Mergus merganser*),

A male Hooded Merganser, as sketched by DW. Often seen in spring, the male bird leaves his mate to raise her brood alone.

which are far less colourful. These are fish ducks, which fly with the bill, head, body, and tail on a horizontal axis, as if someone has drawn a ruler beneath them.

In spring, the male Hooded Merganser is one of our showiest birds. When the white crest is erected on his black head it can be seen for some distance. His black breast shows two black bars on each side; his flanks are brown. The male plays no part in raising the young. For a time in spring, the ducks spend tranquil hours floating and diving on the pond near the house, where they are close enough to be observed with the naked eye.

Later, the female retires to the reeds farther down the creek, where she looks for a cavity in a tree or a fallen log in which to lay her eggs. Over the years, the broods here have numbered, on average, about seven young. In the fall, the little family returns to the pond, where they spend a few days before flying south.

We no longer have fish here, but there are plenty of frogs and water insects, so it is no wonder that the mergansers return year after year. They are always a welcome sight.

HERONS AND KINGFISHERS

Because there is a creek below the house, I often see interesting birds that like to feed there. One favourite is the Belted Kingfisher (*Megaceryle alcyon*), Family *Alcedinidae*, which eats crayfish, salamanders, and mice, all of which we have here. It also favours fish, but we no longer have trout in the pond, so it is out of luck there.

This kingfisher is the only species in Eastern Canada. A handsome bird, it is blue-grey in colour with a crested head. A broad, grey breast-band is part of the plumage of both male and female birds. The female has an additional rusty band, making this one of the few female birds to be more colourful than their mates.

From time to time, herons also come here. My best ever heron sighting involved a Black-crowned Night Heron (*Nycticorax nycticorax*). The adult bird is grey, with a white breast, black back, and black cap. I was fortunate to come across this bird because it is primarily nocturnal, and tends to be heard rather than seen. It flies away from its daytime resting place to feed at dusk.

I enjoy the long daylight hours of summer, when it is possible to fit in an extra walk after dinner. I was walking along the creek bank one evening, when I saw this bird staring into the water. The sun was going down so possibly it had just woken up. I was able to take a long look at the heron, identifying it without difficulty. Fortunately for me, this was an adult bird. Had it been an immature one I doubt if I would have been so sure, for at that stage several of the heron species look rather alike.

The Green Heron (*Butorides striatus*) is a more regular visitor here. When fully adult, this small, dark heron is easy to identify because of its bluish-green back and long neck, which is a deep chestnut colour. When I first saw one, it was perching in a dead tree in the beaver flood. It was obviously alarmed to see me, because it stretched up its neck in a crooked manner, pointing to the sky and putting up the crest on its head. I have seen Green Herons here at other times, but of course it is much easier to identify them when they are standing still than when they are flying.

The Great Blue Heron (*Ardea herodias*) is very common here, especially since there is a heronry a few miles away across country. Some local people call this bird a crane, which is a mistake as cranes belong to a quite different family. Similarly, I've heard many people refer to the birds' nesting colony as a rookery, which is surprising, since we don't have rooks in this part of the world.

This bird is seen here even in winter, for it will stay as long as there is open water. I love to look out on a summer morning to see a Great Blue Heron standing on one leg on the dock, looking hopefully into the water. Not everyone admires this fine bird. "I'd like to shoot the lot of them," a fish farmer told us one day. He had lost too many of his trout to these herons.

The American Bittern (*Botaurus lentiginosus*), with its strange, pumping call, is a stocky brown heron. These also visit Poison Ivy Acres. Although they are well camouflaged, they are common enough in the district, where there is a certain amount of swampy ground. Early one Sunday morning, I was driving past my front fields on my way to church when

Early morning at Poison Ivy Acres. A Great Blue Heron waits patiently for breakfast to appear.

171

A Great Blue Heron returns to the nest. These large birds nest in colonies, known as heronries.

I noticed a bittern standing at the roadside. It was very still and its bill was pointing up towards the sky. This is a typical stance when the bird is at rest, or when danger threatens and it wants to merge in with the scenery. No other traffic was on the road, and no doubt the bird felt the need to conceal itself when it heard my vehicle approaching.

 ## THE GREAT HORNED OWLS

Several species of owls are year-round residents at Poison Ivy Acres. Of these, the Great Horned Owls are most often seen, partly because they hunt by day, and partly because, year after year, they usually return to the same nest, high up in an old pine tree. This tree can be

seen from the house. I have described elsewhere how DW contributed to the building of their sturdy nest and how, later on, Blackie Ryan had a terrifying encounter with one of the owls that was out hunting for food.

    One year, I crossed the creek and walked up to the tree. I was delighted to see two large, white owlets peeping over the edge of the nest. I sat down to watch, and the youngsters stared back, obviously intrigued by this large apparition. Moments later, one of them stood up, stepped out onto a branch and began to walk along it with exaggerated strides, like a child playing "Grandmother's Footsteps." That was when the parent bird swooped into

A pair of Great Horned owlets peer out at the wider world. The young birds are white in colour.

173

action. The mother — or it could equally well have been the father, for both parents feed the young owls — joined her errant child on the branch. A hard slap with a wing sent it scurrying back into the nest to join its sibling. They cowered down, out of sight.

Then it was my turn. The owl flew down, skimming over me closely enough that I could feel the rush of air as she passed. I put up my arms to protect my head but it wasn't necessary. Having delivered a warning, the bird was gone. It probably sensed that I could not have reached the nest.

Two little heads popped up over the edge of the nest. Two pairs of big eyes regarded me with interest. I decided to move on before anything unfortunate happened. I have seen owlets in that nest many times since, but never again have they been compelled to take a closer look at me.

 ## THE SMALLEST OF ALL

Once a year, my mother-in-law used to stay up all night, patiently waiting for her Night-blooming Cereus to come into flower. The blossoms on this cactus appear just once a year, only to fade within hours. For Margaret, seeing this phenomenon was well worth losing sleep over. Equally amazing, perhaps, is that the original plant was brought by her uncle from the American West over one hundred years ago, as a gift for her mother, and it was still thriving. On reaching adulthood, members of the family had taken cuttings from the parent plant to take to their own homes.

I also roam the house during the night hours, but in my case I'm hoping to see a Saw-whet Owl. This miniature owl (*Aegolius acadius*) is not much more than seven inches tall, and because it is nocturnal few people are able to catch a glimpse of it. I've been fortunate enough to see one on several occasions, because it comes to my bird feeders in winter. These owls eat small rodents, which in turn come out at night to pick up seeds that have fallen on the ground.

There are some winters when the bird doesn't appear at all. I have come to the conclusion that the weather has something to do with this. It is more likely to wait near the feeders when there is a crust on the snow, which prevents it from finding prey in open country. When it does come, it is usually in December. Sometimes it appears on successive nights, and I suspect that this means it has been unlucky in catching anything to eat and must return the next night. One year, it actually came in time to be included in the Christmas Bird Count, which was a thrill.

Throughout December 2009, I kept watch for the bird. I must admit that I no longer stay up all night. Usually, it's enough to look out last thing at night and then again just before dawn. There was no sign of the bird, but I was reluctant to give up. Something told me that the weather conditions were right for it to come.

Then, on January the eighth I had my reward! I looked out of my office window at 7:00 a.m. that morning and was delighted to see the Saw-whet Owl perched in the Amur Maple. It remained in place even after the outside light was switched on, enabling me to get a good look at it, but as soon as the sky was fully light it flew off. Sadly, I doubt if it had caught anything because, as I watched, it continued to swivel its head from side to side, occasionally gazing up at me with bright yellow eyes. Would it return? I continued to look out for the remainder of the month, without success.

The Saw-whet Owl derives its name from its song, a note that is repeated as often as one hundred or more times a minute. I have heard this in summer, and years ago, before one of these owls began coming to the house, DW was determined that we would go out and try to spot one. His idea was that we would follow the sound of the bird's hooting until we found it perched in a tree where, with any luck, we could catch a glimpse of it. He reasoned that, since Saw-whet Owls are known to be tame little birds, it might co-operate with us.

Armed with powerful flashlights, we set out in the direction of the back forty, following the bird's calls: *too, too, too, too too!* Muffled curses accompanied this progress, as shrubs barred our way and briars leapt up to catch at our legs. Finally, we arrived at a large oak tree, where the owl had been waiting.

"Switch on your flashlight now," DW whispered. "Slowly, mind!"

The owl was wiser than we were. We soon heard calls coming from some distance away. Was it our bird's mate, or had it simply moved away from us? Alas, our flashlights showed nothing and the bird led us on a merry dance, moving from place to place as we came crashing after it. We were forced to go home, disappointed.

A FACE AT THE WINDOW

During one long-ago spring break, my youngest daughter brought a school friend to stay with us. The pair were sleeping in the guest house, which, before being converted by us, was the hayloft over the barn and horse stable. The children always enjoyed bringing their friends to stay there; it was far enough from the main house for them to play their music without disturbing those who needed their sleep.

There was a bright moon that night, and in the morning the girls reported an eerie happening, in the form of a face at the window. "The thing was peering in at us, and it had whiskers!" they told me. They knew it couldn't have been a cat, since, with the exception of a squirrel, no animal could have scaled the wall beneath that particular window. There was much discussion concerning their phantom visitor.

The next night, the mystery was solved. A Whip-poor-will was found roosting under the little overhang at the door to the building. Field guides say that these birds sleep in the daytime, either on the forest floor or perched on a tree limb, so I was most fortunate to find this one over the door.

In reverse of the way in which Victorian children were supposed to behave, Whip-poor-wills are often heard, but seldom seen, being nocturnal. As for being on the windowsill, Whip-poor-wills eat moths, and probably it was picking off some that had been attracted to the light in the girls' bedroom. And yes, these birds do have large bristles on either side of the beak, so the girls were quite correct in describing what they had seen.

It is a sad fact that the Whip-poor-will population is in decline, and for some years now a lone bird has been heard calling for a mate at Poison Ivy Acres, with no response. Even in the days when these birds may have raised families here, I had no hope of finding where they laid their eggs, for they don't build nests. Their plumage is well camouflaged, and the eggs are hatched on the ground under a tree or shrub, and this place has thousands of such sites.

Being so keen on observing nature, I sometimes have to remind myself that not everyone shares my delight in finding wild things. One way or another, our young friend, a town child, had a distressing time here. When we were walking down to the creek she was alarmed when a snake crossed her path. The poor creature was so desperate to avoid us that it slithered away at a great rate.

"It's only a garter snake," I explained to our visitor. "It's quite harmless, and in any case, it's gone now."

She gave me what my grandmother would have called an old-fashioned look.

"Where there's one, there may be more!" she told me, with a shudder.

That statement has been adopted by our family, being quoted on all suitable occasions. In fact, it's a good maxim to remember, especially when a deer leaps out in front of your car when you are driving at night. They seldom travel alone.

A BARRED OWL AT THE FEEDER

What a surprise it was to see a Barred Owl (*Strix varia*) at the feeder that morning! I happened to look out of the dormer window in my upstairs office and there it was, perched on the high wooden wall that formed part of our bird feeder complex at that time. Nearby there are two large, flat boulders topped with marble slabs that were used to support page frames in the newspaper office, back in the linotype days. This is where we put out seeds for the birds, on what are possibly the only marble bird feeders in the township. It beats plastic every time!

I noticed at once that this large owl had big brown eyes, which immediately identified it as a Barred Owl. Apart from the Barn Owl (*Tyto alba*), which we do not have in our area, this is our only brown-eyed owl. All the rest have yellow eyes.

This was a rare sighting because they are not seed-eaters. It must have come there hoping to find smaller birds, or perhaps rodents that had come out to feast on seeds that had fallen to the ground. The Barred Owl is common enough, and I have often heard it hooting down in the swamp. *Hoohoo-hoohoo, hoohoo- hoohooaw!* However, it is largely nocturnal, which is another reason why it is seldom seen.

We needed a photo of this. Otherwise, who would believe me? I dashed downstairs to find DW, who was in his office at the other end of the house. Delighted, he jumped up at once, reaching for his cameras. He always kept at least two Leicas loaded with film, one with black-and-white, which he preferred, the other for producing colour slides. Digital cameras were unheard of back then, and he probably wouldn't have liked them anyway. He did all his own darkroom work for his black-and-white photos, which I'm sure gave him more satisfaction than producing computerized pictures would have done.

He looked out of the living-room window to make sure that the owl was still in place. Now came a problem. If he went outside, the owl would be frightened off. For the same reason, we didn't dare to open a window. The closest he could get to the owl was the south-facing window in the kitchen, but now there was another problem. Between that window and the owl there was the conservatory, then another large expanse of glass, and DW was reluctant to step out there in case the bird heard the door opening. Also, since the bird was swivelling its neck from side to side, in the manner of all owls when hunting, he was afraid that it would notice the movement, or at least see his shadow.

A Barred Owl at the bird feeder. These brown-eyed owls are primarily nocturnal, so observing this one was a rare treat.

"I'm going to have to shoot it from inside the kitchen," he muttered, as he fastened a telephoto lens onto the camera. "I don't think the result will be too great, but this is too good a chance to miss."

As it turned out, the result was very good indeed, which is saying something when you consider that the photo was taken through two layers of glass, with another room in between. I can't recall it now, but I expect that he used a polaroid lens.

The Barred Owl is the largest of the species without ear tufts that is found on Poison Ivy Acres. It belongs to the Family *Trigidae*, or True Owls. The slightly smaller Hawk Owl has come here on rare occasions, and the tiny Saw-whet has been resident here for some years. A large representative of the "eared" owls, which have tufts on their heads, is the Great Horned Owl, which lives close to the house. That bird is much easier to spot than the Barred Owl because it hunts during the day.

A Hawk Owl is a rare visitor to the district. This crow-sized owl hunts by day, giving the birdwatcher a good opportunity to observe it.

The Audubon Society Field Guide to North American Birds states that the Barred Owl "is seen only by those who seek it out in its dark retreat ... there it rests quietly during the day, coming out at night to feed."[1] That being the case, I consider us extremely lucky to have seen the bird so close to home, and getting a good photo of it was little short of a miracle.

 ## THE OSPREY'S LUNCH

The Osprey (*Pandion haliaetus*) is one of the more fascinating birds to have visited Poison Ivy Acres. Sometimes known as a fish hawk, it is a large brown-backed bird with a white belly and a wingspan of five to six feet. The best field marks are its black cheek and wrist patches, and the fact that the bird usually flies with a crook in its wings. It hunts for prey by hovering on beating wings before plunging into the water feet first. It is fascinating to watch this bird flying away with a fish held in its talons, looking like a small torpedo.

When we had trout in the pond near the house, an Osprey could sometimes be seen perching in a dead tree nearby, waiting for the chance to strike. This was in contrast to a Great Blue Heron, which spent many a patient hour on the dock for the same purpose, standing on one leg while it waited.

Although they have been said to nest on the ground, more often than not Ospreys build their huge, untidy nests high above *terra firma*, using tall trees or even telephone poles for the purpose. In some parts of Ontario, nesting platforms have been erected to encourage these birds to raise their families in safe sites.

Ospreys have yet to nest at Poison Ivy Acres, but I did have an interesting experience with one a few years back. There had been a power outage of several days' duration, with the result that everything in our freezer had defrosted. Of this food, there was only so much that we could eat and the rest had to be thrown out, including a soggy package of cod fillets. I put it out on the lawn expecting that a raccoon might enjoy it, and then went indoors to wash my hands.

I happened to glance up at the mirror over the washbasin when a flash of white crossed my line of vision. It was obviously a large bird so I ran out to see what it was. Lo and behold, it was an Osprey, happily gulping down bits of cod. It had appeared out of nowhere; it certainly hadn't been nearby when I'd gone outside earlier.

---

1.   *Audubon Society Field Guide to North American Birds*, 635.

An Osprey returns to the nest, where its mate awaits. Note the fish grasped in its talons.

It never ceases to amaze me how birds manage to spot food from so far away. Yes, fish-eating birds know enough to check out creeks and ponds, and seed-eaters come to our bird feeders out of habit, expecting to find nourishment there, but what about the birds who come across food by chance, such as Turkey Vultures spotting roadkill? Do they have a highly developed sense of smell?

How was it that an Osprey, who hadn't been seen in the neighbourhood for a long time, was there to snap up the cod within minutes of it being put out? Just one of many unexplained miracles in the world of birdwatching, I guess.

 ## A GREAT WHITE BIRD

Each September, for some years now, I've caught a quick glimpse of a large white bird when climbing the hill to our dog cemetery. This little graveyard is perched high above the creek, giving a commanding view of the beaver meadow below. My sudden appearance has flushed the bird out of its perch in a clump of trees, where I suppose it has been on the lookout for prey. For a long time, I couldn't decide what it was. I guessed that it could be a Gyrfalcon (*Falco rusticolos*) in its white phase, yet a Gyrfalcon, a bird of the Arctic, is an extremely rare visitor to this part of Canada.

On the other hand, an Osprey is also about that size, and they, too, occasionally visit my home, showing their white underparts when they fly up. As I happened to be standing well below the bird, I could not see if it had the Osprey's dark back or black wrist patches.

It has to be said that these two birds are very different from each other in appearance. Also, their flight patterns are different. Falcons have pointed wings and long tails. Ospreys will hover in the air and they fly with a crook in their wings. Any keen birdwatcher should be able to tell the difference at a glance.

In my defence, I have to say that on each occasion the bird quickly disappeared into the thicket and did not come out again. I had no chance of identifying any field marks. On the other hand, this was not typical Osprey behaviour. Such birds can most often be seen perching on a solitary treetop, overlooking water, where they hope to find fish. I mentally filed my sighting away as a possible Gyrfalcon and kept my thoughts to myself. I hesitate to tell other people about a rare sighting unless it has been authenticated by a second birder.

In the Arctic, there are three different colour morphs for Gyrfalcons: black, grey, and white. Each September, I went to the dog cemetery in the hope of seeing the bird again and making a positive identification, and each year I caught a glimpse of white but nothing more. With no idea how long a white phase would last, I couldn't say if my autumn visitor was the same bird or not. By now I was sure that it must be a Gyrfalcon, and I longed to be able to make a positive identification.

In April 2007, my wish was granted! It was a lovely day, and spring was in the air. The sun was shining and the sky was a cloudless blue. I was standing on the township road outside my gate when I noticed a large, white bird flying in the general direction of the dogs' graveyard, which is a mile or so in from the gate. A Gyrfalcon!

It flew in wide circles over the creek. It must have noticed me because it zoomed in and made a couple of circuits right over my head. It came down so low that I could see its shadow on the ground at my feet. It then soared into the sky several times, displaying that characteristic falcon silhouette. The bird was truly magnificent with the sun shining on it.

I reported this to Jim, who writes the bird column in our local newspaper. In return he told me that on the following day, another reader had seen two very white falcon-like birds circling over the town, twelve miles from my home. She had noted that they continued their soaring for most of the afternoon. She had noted black tips on their wings, an important field mark of the Gyrfalcon.

"Everything comes to him who waits" was a favourite saying of my late father. Certainly my experience that April day was something worth waiting for.

CANADA GEESE

Goosey, goosey gander,
Whither will you wander?

One sunny spring morning, when I was walking out to the mailbox, I spotted a little family out for a stroll. A gander and his mate, walking on either side of their three small goslings, seemed to have not a care in the world, but no doubt they were ready to spring into action if anything threatened their brood. I wondered where they had nested, although I suspected that it was somewhere deep in the patch of swamp that lay between my hayfields and the edge of the township road. Some time earlier, I'd found a goose egg on that same road, which had probably been stolen by a crow and deposited there. Another egg lay floating in the water. A day later, pieces of empty shell bore silent witness to the fact that something had enjoyed a tasty meal. Raccoons also like eggs, but they consume them on the spot rather than carrying them away.

Some Canada Geese come in for a landing. They are among the first birds to return to Poison Ivy Acres in the spring, and the last to leave in the fall.

The placid behaviour of the strolling geese was quite different from the aggressive attitude of a gander we encountered some years ago. During the spring flood, DW and I were canoeing down a creek a few miles from home. As we rounded a bend, we noticed a large, high nest on which a watchful goose was sitting. This nest seemed to have been built on some earlier structure, possibly a beaver house, but we didn't stop to examine it, for a very angry gander was coming straight for us, flying low and uttering unwelcoming noises.

Canada Geese enjoy walking across country, especially when they have their goslings with them. Here, a trio search for food on a summer day.

"Get ready!" DW roared, just in case I hadn't noticed anything amiss. It was all very well for him, kneeling in the stern. I was in the bow, a ready target for our feathered enemy. Talk about a sitting duck! Paddle raised, I held my breath. I was reminded of those religious warnings that used to be displayed on billboards in Wales during my childhood. PREPARE TO MEET THY DOOM! However, the gander veered aside at the last moment, and our little craft shot downstream, unmolested.

The Canada Goose (*Branta canadensis*) seems to arouse conflicting emotions in the hearts of Canadians. For one thing, these birds congregate in great numbers along some of our waterways, such as the tourist areas along the St. Lawrence River, leaving a great deal of mess in their wake. In our area, farmers quite naturally resent having their freshly seeded land invaded by a hungry, cackling mob.

On the other hand, who among us has not thrilled to the sight of a skein of geese, honking their way across the autumn sky as they prepare to fly south? Summer is gone, and winter will soon be here, they seem to say. Similarly, their return in the spring is a happy reminder of glorious summer days to come. Other than the beloved robin, there are few birds whose arrival is more welcome. And it is a special treat if a Snow Goose can be spotted among its more everyday cousins.

Canada Geese mate for life. It wrings my heart when a goose is shot during hunting season and its mate flies over my property, calling mournfully and desperately looking for its lost partner. A year or two back, someone reported to our local newspaper that a dead goose had been found lying on a frozen lake, while its mate stayed nearby, apparently conducting a vigil. We can all relate to this behaviour, which seems to mimic the human condition. If only we could know what was going through the creature's mind at such a time! Cats and dogs are known to fret and mourn when a housemate dies, whether it be animal or human, so it surely it can't be fanciful to imagine that a bird can grieve as well?

 ## NATURE HEADLINES

When you pick up your newspaper nowadays you invariably see some nasty headlines. Come to think of it, I've seen some sights in our neighbourhood that would rate some alarmist headings. Consider these:

MASKED BANDIT KILLS BYSTANDER
ROW OF BODIES DISCOVERED ON LONELY ROAD
FATHER ABANDONS WIFE, TWELVE CHILDREN
MOTHER FOSTERS ABANDONED BABY

Makes you wonder what the world is coming to, doesn't it? You may be interested to know that we didn't call the police, despite the fact that all these episodes happened right here at Poison Ivy Acres. With both of us having been weekly newspaper editors, it's hard not to think in terms of headlines.

The masked bandit was a Northern Shrike that sat in a tree beside our bird feeders, looking most businesslike in its black eye mask. It wasn't interested in the seeds and suet we provided; its idea was to prey on smaller birds. There is something eerie about a wild creature that preys on its own kind. I can remember feeling quite indignant one winter at the sight of a Cooper's Hawk picking off purple finches at a feeder. However, this is all part of nature, and shrikes and hawks must eat to survive. I've read that a shrike will sometimes impale its kill on a thorn or a piece of barbed wire, thereby storing it safely while it continues to hunt. I have always hoped to come across this phenomenon, but I haven't been lucky yet.

It was DW who discovered the bodies in the lane: a group of dead rodents, all laid out in a careful row. Judging by the tracks and droppings we found, this was the work of a Red Fox. We guessed that this was a dog fox, which had been disturbed in the act of collecting enough food to feed its mate and young family.

I have learned that foxes are quite inquisitive. They will watch people to see what they are doing, and occasionally, when I've left a trail of footprints in the snow, I've gone back later to find that a fox has followed in my tracks. This has happened with wolves as well. Perhaps this is a defence mechanism, with the animals wanting to know what I've been doing, or maybe it is a way of defining their territory into which an alien species has trespassed.

Each April, we see a pair of Hooded Mergansers on the pond below the house. The male has a showy black-and-white head, which is beautiful to see. I like to study these birds while I can, for, after mating with the female, the male soon disappears, leaving his partner to raise their family alone. Hooded Mergansers are cavity nesters and ours always choose the same area, where a beaver flood has left many dead and decaying trees beside the creek. Sometimes, on a summer evening, I have seen the mother and her large family swimming

"Not today, thank you!" A Tree Swallow peers crossly at a visitor to her entryway.

among the cattails, and in the fall we have often been delighted by the sight of half a dozen young mergansers hunting for crayfish.

Cowbirds are notorious for laying their eggs in the nests of other birds and leaving the unfortunate foster mother to raise their young. The male cowbirds are quite bold, but the drabber females flit quietly through the branches, not advertising their presence to the host females.

One year a Black-capped Chickadee received one of these unwanted foster children in her nest close to the house. How she managed to deal with her giant charge is anybody's guess: the alien was twice her size. More often than not, the chickadees nest in our bluebird boxes, where the cowbirds can't reach them because the entrance holes are too small.

The behaviour of birds and humans seem to run on parallel courses. During the winter of 1987–88, we had a great many Common Redpolls and Pine Siskins at a hanging feeder, and there was one very fat siskin bully who refused to share. He constantly attacked the other birds with beak and claw, scolding and complaining loudly. I'm sure that teachers have seen similar sights among their human charges in the schoolyard.

We know that in war, and among primitive societies, sentries or lookouts are used to warn groups of impending danger. This seems to happen with flocks of birds, too. One winter, we had a flock of about sixty Snow Buntings who stayed with us for several months. They perched in a tall maple near the house, eyeing the seed that we spread for them on the ground.

Each day, these visitors from the tundra watched and waited for an hour or more until, at last, a single bird emerged from the flock, inspected the seed, and immediately returned to the group. After that, they descended together in a cloud. Snow Buntings are group-oriented, and when one bird flies up from the ground, they all do, looking like a shower of snowflakes. In their wide-open northern habitat, it is easier for them to see approaching danger, but at Poison Ivy Acres there are few open spaces. This is probably why they so seldom visit us, preferring fields elsewhere in the township.

I once saw a similar phenomenon in the fall, when the trees were filled with hundreds of male Red-winged Blackbirds preparing to migrate. (Males and females migrate at different times.) First there was a great chattering from these birds, then came a sudden silence as a lone bird called. This was repeated over and over again. It was almost like a scene from a Hitchcock movie.

How I wish I knew what was happening there. Was it a disgruntled bird, out of step with the others, or was the lone blackbird acting as a sort of cheerleader, giving travel directions to the rest? Was it part of the mystery of migration? I shall never know, but no matter what we humans do, nature seems to have thought of it first.

A DIZZY WOODPECKER

From time to time, a bird flies into a window here, stunning itself, if not worse. Several times Ruffed Grouse have been found on the ground with their necks broken, and Hairy Woodpeckers have also been known to crash into the glass. This is one of the penalties of living in a house surrounded by trees. I suppose the birds see the foliage reflected in the glass and assume they can keep flying.

One morning, a male Hairy Woodpecker hit my bedroom window with such a thump that the sound brought me from my computer in the next room. Peering out, I saw that the poor bird had fallen into the lilacs below and was clutching a branch for dear life. As I watched, it sank backwards in slow motion, attached to the shrub with its strong feet, until it was lying horizontally. Its eyes closed slowly and I was sure that it was in its death throes. After a while I went back to work.

An hour later, I went to check on it, and there it was, still lying on its back, supported only by its talons. I was sure that rigor mortis must have set in by now. Yet another hour passed, and the bird was still attached to the lilacs. Then, suddenly, it gave a shudder and righted itself. Eventually it flew away, looking rather groggy. Some time later I saw it attacking the suet ball at the feeder. What a miraculous recovery!

Some years earlier, a female Hairy Woodpecker had hit that same window. Donning leather gloves, DW went out and picked up the bird, which was lying on the ground as if dead. He meant to cradle it in his hands in the hope that the warmth would eventually revive it. The woodpecker came to her senses in a hurry and began to jab at him with her strong beak, making a hole in his glove. As gently as possible, he put her back on the ground. A woodpecker that can bore a hole in the trunk of a maple tree can inflict damage in a hurry on a well-meaning human!

Seven species of woodpecker, members of the Family *Picidae*, have been seen at Poison Ivy Acres. The Hairy Woodpecker (*Picoides villosus*) and the tiny Downy Woodpecker (*Picoides pubescens*) come to the bird feeders all winter. Although they drill for insects, they also like the suet and sunflower seeds I provide. When eating the suet, they lean backwards in typical woodpecker fashion, supported by their feet. But to get at the seeds that I throw out from the window of my upstairs office, they lie on their bellies on the sloping roof of the laundry room.

My favourite is the magnificent Pileated Woodpecker (*Dryocopus pileatus*), which is a spectacular crow-sized bird with a large red crest. Sometimes I catch a glimpse of one in the

A Hairy Woodpecker takes a rest. These are among the most frequent visitors to the feeders in winter.

bush, but more often it advertises its presence with an enormous oblong hole in a tree. The Pileated Woodpeckers usually raise two young, somewhere in the neighbourhood.

Two rare birds have very occasionally been spotted on this property. They are the Northern Three-toed Woodpecker (*Picoides tridactylus*, formerly known as the Ladder-backed Woodpecker) and the Black-backed (Arctic) Three-toed Woodpecker (*Picoides articus*). The males of these species have yellow caps and barred sides. One winter, I thought for a brief moment that one of these had come to the feeder, but the plain white back of the bird proclaimed it to be an immature Hairy Woodpecker with a yellowish cap that had not yet become red. In any case, the Three-toed Woodpeckers have only been spotted among the tall trees beside the lane, at some distance from the house.

The summer woodpeckers are much more colourful birds. The male Yellow-bellied Sapsucker (*Sphrapicus varius*) has a red cap and throat, while the Yellow-shafted Flicker (*Colaptes auratus*) is a handsome bird indeed. Recognizable in flight by its white rump, this is a colourful bird when viewed close up. It has a brown back, a spotted yellow breast with a black "necklace," and a red cap. The male has a prominent black "moustache." Flickers often

A female Yellow-shafted Flicker. These birds are our only brown-backed woodpeckers.

invade my lawn, turning their heads on one side to listen as they search for ants, leaving holes behind for me to fill up.

So far, I have never seen a Red-headed Woodpecker (*Melanerpes erythrocephalus*) at Poison Ivy Acres, although this rare bird has very occasionally been seen in other parts of the county. This is the only eastern woodpecker with an entirely red head. When I was writing my bird column, I occasionally received a call from some excited reader, claiming to have seen a Red-headed Woodpecker, but investigation usually proved that it was one of the species mentioned earlier. The birds they had observed did have red markings on their heads, but they were not *the* Red-headed Woodpecker!

 ## THE WOUNDED BLACKBIRD

One morning during the first week of May, I caught a glimpse of something red in a spruce tree near my office window. A closer look proved — or so I thought at first — that it was a male Red-winged Blackbird trying to attract a mate. The red epaulettes, or wing patches, were puffed up so as to be visible from several yards away.

But wait a minute! Now the bird seemed to have a large red patch on the back of its head, something like the Common Flicker, although this was definitely a blackbird. Puzzled, I ran for the binoculars, but the movement inside the window probably frightened the bird, because it flew away before I could get them focused.

I had to leave for an appointment, so it was some hours before I could look for the bird again, but it did not reappear. Sometimes after a period of bad weather — and goodness knows we had our share of that in those first months of 2008 — a rare bird will appear, blown off course and desperate for rest and food. But as far as I know there is no Red-headed Blackbird, or at least not in our part of the world!

The following day, the bird was feeding on the ground outside my kitchen window where I had thrown some seeds out for the newly arrived White-crowned and White-throated Sparrows. Now was my chance! Grabbing the downstairs field glasses I hastily adjusted them, and gave a gasp of horror. The poor bird had a huge gouge out of the back of its neck, and that was the red I had seen. Its eyes were closed, and it looked as if it had been blinded.

This sad sight reminded me of the time when one of my hens had been attacked by the rest of the flock and deprived of most of its feathers. In this case, however, the other birds around it displayed no animosity. Grackles, cowbirds, and other Red-winged Blackbirds foraged quietly alongside it, paying no attention to it at all.

I realized then that it had probably fallen victim to the immature Cooper's Hawk that had been hunting close to the house all winter. It had picked off a Blue Jay and a few chickadees, leaving discarded feathers and a small pool of blood in the snow. It was either that, or the Great Horned Owl, which is nesting across the creek at the time of writing.

For three days, there was no further sign of the wounded bird. I kept throwing seed on the ground and then, suddenly, he was back. One bright eye was open, so he still had some sight. After a few days had passed, it looked as if the damage to his neck had begun to heal. The poor bird was teetering rather stiffly as it picked up the seeds; no doubt he was feeling some pain. I hoped that he could manage to stay safe from then on.

For two days in a row, I went outside, only to find a few blue feathers on the ground in different spots. It seemed that the hawk was still having some hunting success. I realize that nature has designed it to be carnivorous, so I really shouldn't have felt upset when it managed to find a meal. However, I certainly hoped that it wouldn't pick off the little pair of Red-breasted Nuthatches that are among my favourite visitors. It probably prefers something with more meat on it, such as my poor wounded blackbird.

ANY PORT IN A STORM

The wind doth blow
And we shall have snow
And what will the robin do then, poor thing?

My grandmother used to quote this old rhyme to me when I was a child, and I always felt so sorry for the poor robin. I'm still sorry for robins, even though I'm thinking about a different species of bird now, in a faraway place. It seems that we always have at least one snowstorm after they return to Poison Ivy Acres, and they don't have a hope of digging up worms in that situation. At times, I have seen them reduced to eating juniper berries as a result. On the other hand, a good storm, particularly in summer, sometimes blows the birds off course, and if I'm lucky, something rare or uncommon arrives at Poison Ivy Acres to delight me.

But where do birds go when they need to take shelter in a hurry? I found out one summer day, when a violent thunderstorm blew up suddenly and I was far from the house. Everyone knows that you have to stay away from trees during a thunderstorm. It is foolish to stand next to one because it might get struck by lightning, and you along with it. However, if you happen to be in the bush, as I was, there isn't much choice.

Fearing that I might get battered by the torrential rain, I crawled under a giant spruce, whose lower branches swept the ground. Kneeling there, I found some protection, and when I raised my head I saw that several small birds — chickadees and sparrows — had the same idea. They were perching in the lower branches and they didn't seem unduly threatened by my sudden appearance. Perhaps my company was the lesser of two evils, because they all stayed where they were.

As for the danger of getting struck by lightning, that can happen anywhere. An almighty crash at Poison Ivy Acres during one summer storm was heard by neighbours a long distance away. Lightning had struck the well, damaging the motor. I have heard that lightning follows the course of water, and this incident seems to lend credence to that theory.

"Never sit on the toilet during a thunderstorm," one elderly woman advised me, making me smile, but then she had grown up having to use an outdoor privy on the farm, located beside a giant oak tree. Her experience might have been something different altogether.

One January day, I saw an unusual sight. There was a wicked wind and the snow was drifting badly. In some places the road was absolutely bare and in others it was knee-high in the white stuff. At times visibility was almost nil. Buffeted by the cruel wind, I was waiting at the mailbox, having gone out early to post some letters, and I was longing for the mail lady to arrive so I could turn and head for home.

Suddenly, I noticed a large bird flying towards me, travelling at some speed, just three or four feet above the ground. It was a Great Blue Heron that seemed to be disoriented by the wind. It didn't appear to notice me as it went racing past like a grey wraith. It was probably going to the nearby lake, if indeed it made it that far. I guessed that it was flying so low in an attempt to avoid being blown backwards by the strong gusts of wind. Similarly, I have crouched over the handlebars of my bicycle, to avoid being blown backwards.

These herons stay in the district as long as there is open water, and they are often seen on the Christmas Bird Count. February usually sees their return, so I can't say if this particular bird was leaving or returning. In any event, it was a sight to see.

FASCINATING SPARROWS

I'm aware that some people think that sparrows are ordinary little birds, without much to recommend them. Apart from the time of the Christmas Bird Count, when House Sparrows and American Tree Sparrows usually make the list, people seldom send in reports of sparrows to our local bird columnists. That is too bad, for by ignoring the sparrows they miss the chance to find out more about these fascinating little birds.

As I glance out of my window on this January day, I see the cheerful little American Tree Sparrows (*Spizella arborea*), which are hopping forward to take their share of the sunflower seeds I've put out. This bird has a reddish brown cap and two white wing bars. Its breast is pale, apart from a dark spot in the centre, which is often referred to as a stickpin. It is that mark that differentiates it from a summer visitor, the Chipping Sparrow (*Spizella passerine*). For this reason the tree sparrow is nicknamed "the winter chippy."

Chipping Sparrows have a black and a white line through the eye, and a bright rufous cap. These birds are very common here, and they have been known to nest in the bluebird boxes. I have to keep a close eye on the tree sparrows, whose time here never seems to overlap with the Chipping Sparrows. It seems that the tree sparrows can be here one day, and then I wake up the next morning to find the Chipping Sparrows are here in their place.

Some very handsome sparrows come to the feeder complex in the spring, eating seed on the ground. The White-crowned Sparrow (*Zonotrichia leucophrys*) is usually the first of these, a few of them usually arriving amid a flock of juncos. Then comes the White-throated Sparrow (*Zonotrichia albicollis*) with its sweet spring calls, and the heavily streaked Song Sparrow (*Melospiza melodia*) can soon be seen and heard nearby. The Field Sparrow (*Spizella pusilla*) can often be noticed at the upper edge of the lane, where junipers and other small shrubs grow. It can be hard to distinguish from the other rusty-capped sparrows unless one can get a look at its pinkish beak. It is also hard to tell the difference between the Swamp Sparrow (*Melospia georgiana*) and other sparrows, so it's very likely that this species is far more common here than I realize. I shall have to make a point of studying these look-alikes in future.

However, the Vesper Sparrow (*Pooecetes gramineus*) is easy to identify because of its white tail coverts, and I'm surprised that more people are not aware of it. An early arrival in spring, it doesn't come near the feeders, but seems to spend its time flying in and out of hedgerows and ditches where my outer fields border the township roads. This bird nests in open spaces on the ground, which is why I most often see it near the hayfields.

My undoubted favourite is the Fox Sparrow (*Passerella iliaca*), which arrives in the fall on its way to winter quarters in the southern United States from its breeding ground in northern Canada. This is a large, heavily streaked sparrow with a rufous tail. Each year, a solitary bird, or sometimes two, can be seen from my kitchen window as they poke their way among the leaves that have fallen from the Amur Maple, searching for food. I am charmed by the way they kick up the leaves with their feet while giving a backward hop.

By far, my most exciting sighting, however, came when a Golden-crowned Sparrow (*Zonotrichia atricapilla*) arrived at the house several years ago. I wasn't the only local bird-watcher to report seeing one that late summer, and fortunately I wasn't alone when I spotted it here. Whenever I see a rare or accidental bird, I hesitate to claim the sighting unless at least one other person has confirmed it. I think there must have been some special reason, such as unusual weather conditions, for the arrival of these birds, for their usual range is farther west, and I have never seen one since.

The Golden-crowned Sparrow is rather like the White-crowned Sparrow in appearance, except that the adult bird has a dull yellow central crown, heavily bordered in black. In its native habitat, the bird breeds in willow and alder scrub, both of which are found at Poison Ivy Acres. However, when I saw it, the bird was perching on the outer branches of the spruce outside the living-room window, where it obligingly remained for some time so that we could observe it.

It was one of those experiences that birdwatchers look forward to for years. I must say, however, that sparrows of all shapes and sizes are most welcome here. In all their infinite variety, they enliven the landscape, they harm nobody, and they provide the birdwatcher with the opportunity of sharpening his identification skills. Sparrows deserve more recognition than they currently receive.

 ## HUMMINGBIRD TALES

I think of hummingbirds, Family *Trochilidae*, as little miracles. Although they are so tiny, little more than three inches long, they are able to fly thousands of miles while migrating. There are more than three hundred species worldwide, but here in eastern Canada we have just one, the Ruby-throated Hummingbird (*Archilochus colubris*). This bird winters in Mexico and Central America.

The male bird has a glowing red throat, a bright metallic green back, and a forked tail. His mate is more soberly dressed, with a blunt tail. Hummingbirds have long bills like needles, which allow them to sip the nectar from the red blossoms they favour. I am fortunate enough to see these miniature birds each summer. Like other bird fanciers, I put out a hummingbird feeder filled with sweet red syrup. The birds usually arrive before my flowering crabapple trees bloom, and they need something to sustain them. The same is true in the fall, when they are preparing to fly south. They always go to investigate the scarlet runners in the garden, but I doubt they can get inside the curiously-shaped blossoms.

The trouble is that ants also enjoy the syrup! They get into the feeders and drown. Fed up with this one summer, I hung the feeder from the middle of the clothesline, several feet about the ground. The birds were happy enough with that. The ants just had to work a little harder. One end of the line is attached to a tall basswood tree. The ants travelled up the trunk and walked along the wire in a hungry procession. I found this amazing. The instinct to survive affects ants in remarkable ways.

It's different with the hummingbirds. They are attracted to the colour red, apparently being conditioned to think that it leads to a source of food. One day, I stepped outside wearing a red apron and was immediately spotted by a hummingbird who rushed at me, only to be disappointed. I'm only thankful that I wasn't wearing lipstick at the time. I dread to think what might have happened!

Hummingbirds seldom stay still. They hover when they feed, and their wing motion is so rapid as to appear blurred. I once had the privilege of watching one of them perching absolutely still. We were having a violent rainstorm, one of those downpours that quickly fills the water barrels, and I happened to glance out the window overlooking the clothesline. The other end is attached to the wall of the house, underneath the eaves. The little bird was perched on the line, completely motionless, sheltered by the overhanging roof. I was glad to have the opportunity of studying it in detail.

The summer of 2009 was very wet, but we did suffer a heat wave early in the season. Having come home from shopping, I parked my car at the back door while I carried my groceries inside. Suddenly, Rufus jumped up at the kitchen window, making low cries of indignation. On going out to see what he was looking at, I saw a male hummingbird, furiously attacking the car window. Although this bird has a delicate little beak, I was afraid that the glass might crack, so I had to chase him away. I assume it could see its reflection in the glass and was trying to drive away what it believed was another male invading its territory.

It is my hope that one day I shall find the nest of these summer visitors. I do want to see the eggs, which are only about the size of a pea. There are lots of shrubs and small trees near the house, so I live in hope!

 # ROBINS

If there is one Canadian bird that everyone can recognize without a doubt, it is the robin. The American Robin (*Turdus migratorius*) is a well-known summer visitor to eastern Canada, in urban and rural areas alike.

Actually, the bird is a thrush, a member of the Family *Turdidae*. The male has a dark head and back, and a distinctive red breast, while his mate is lighter in colour. The juvenile robin has a speckled breast with a reddish wash. When the first settlers came from the British Isles and parts of Europe to North America, they named this bird after the smaller robin redbreast of their homeland.

When I was writing a bird column, readers took great delight in trying to be the first to spot this harbinger of spring, or to hear its sweet song. And why not? Our winters here are so harsh that any sign that spring is near is welcome indeed.

Unfortunately, the robins often arrive at Poison Ivy Acres before winter is truly finished, and they find themselves suffering the stress of a late snowstorm. I can recall one April when my flowering crabapple trees were already in blossom and we received several inches of snow. The robins were here, but there were no berries because there had been a drought the previous autumn, and the ground was still too hard for them to find worms. No insects had yet appeared because of the cold, and the outlook for the robins' survival was grim. I raided my store cupboards and found a few raisins, which I hoped they'd enjoy. Other wild creatures were enthusiastic about this treasure, so I don't know if the timid robins had a share.

Each year, several pairs of robins nest around the house, under the eaves of the guest house, and beneath the beams in the open woodshed. Sadly, packs of marauding crows usually rob the nests while the poor robins try in vain to fend them off. Bright blue eggshells — robin's-egg blue — litter the ground as a result.

Robins will also nest in a tree or shrub, and last season one pair decided to build in one of the tall spruces outside my bedroom window. In due course, I saw the birds going in and out, so no doubt some of the eggs had hatched. An average of four eggs are laid, incubated by the female alone for eleven to fourteen days.

It seems to me that the robins get excited when they hear me revving up the lawn mower. As soon as I have completed the job, they swoop down onto the nice green grass, which gives them better access to the worms that lie beneath the surface. They relish a wet day, when several of them can be seen hopping about on the damp grass, searching for a meal.

Yes, these cheerful birds are very welcome visitors, and it is a sad day when they gather together and fly away. They must leave in the night, for it's a case of "here today, gone tomorrow." A morning eventually comes when I wake up to find that not a robin can be seen, for they have embarked on their long journey to Mexico. Sometimes, one solitary robin will stay behind to be included in the Christmas Bird Count, and nobody knows why this happens. Was it too weak to make the trip? Rejected by the other birds? Luckily, people who operate bird feeders are always willing to give a lonely robin a helping hand.

WHISKY JACK AND SPRUCE GROUSE

Once in a while, I'm lucky enough to see birds that are rare visitors to Poison Ivy Acres, although they are common residents farther north. One of these is the Canada Jay, also known as the Grey Jay (*Perisoreus canadensis*). This bird is much the size of our more common Blue Jay, and a little larger than a robin. As its name suggests, this jay is grey with a partial black cap and a white throat. In apperance, it resembles a giant chickadee.

Familiar to lumbermen and others who work in the northern woods, this extremely tame bird has many names, camp robber and whisky jack among them. Where there is food in the offing, there you will find this jay.

In my case, I have occasionally noticed a whisky jack on the Amur Maple, waiting for seeds to be thrown out. DW often photographed such birds when he was staying in a camp across the Ottawa River in Pontiac County. To add to the fun, he persuaded his friend Ted to hold a toothpick between his lips with a piece of cheese on it, and within minutes a jay came and snatched it away.

I have had my own adventures with a Spruce Grouse (*Canachites canadensis*), Family *Tetraonidae*. This bird is also very tame, almost to the point of stupidity. While that is good

A whisky jack zooms in to take a piece of cheese from DW's friend, Ted. These tame little birds readily accept food from friendly birdwatchers.

news for the birdwatcher, it leaves the bird open to capture by predators. One day, I drove home from town, planning to park the car at the back door while I unloaded my groceries, but when I arrived in the top yard, I found my way barred by a male Spruce Grouse. He strutted about in front of me, quite unconcerned, and short of mowing him down there was no way I could drive on. I got out and clapped my hands, and that made him move, although he showed no sign of panic. Rising and landing, rising and landing, he finally disappeared into the long grass and I was able to complete my trip, delighted with what I had seen.

The Spruce Grouse is a little smaller than my resident Ruffed Grouse. The male bird is a handsome fellow, with a conspicuous black breast and throat and white barring on his sides. There is a chestnut-coloured band on the tail. In common with other birds that nest on the ground, the female is more drably attired, being a dark rusty brown.

The first time I saw a Spruce Grouse here I was quite excited. It was a male bird, wandering about outside my kitchen window. I grabbed the binoculars at once to verify this sighting, although it was hardly necessary because the bird's distinctive plumage gave it away. He stayed long enough for me to take in all the details before he retreated to the shelter of the tall spruces, a couple of yards from the window. Over the next few days, he appeared repeatedly, seldom venturing far from any of the spruces.

The following year a pair of these birds arrived together and remained for several days. Winter was winding down, and I was hopeful that they might nest here, but perhaps that was too much to expect. Nevertheless, seeing them here was a delight, and I hope that Spruce Grouse will continue to come to Poison Ivy Acres.

DOWN THE HATCH!

Anyone who has a wood stove will be familiar with the spring ritual that involves rescuing a bird from the stovepipes. Although our chimneys are properly cowled, starlings always manage to worm their way into what they think will provide a suitable nesting site. Possibly our most unpopular bird visitor, the European Starling (*Sturnus vulgaris*) is a speckled bird with a yellow beak. The problem is that the starling is a cavity nester, which is why it's drawn to our chimneys with unfailing regularity.

My heart sinks whenever I go into the workshop on a spring morning and I hear bird-song coming from inside the stovepipe. The starling sings so sweetly in captivity that it almost breaks the listener's heart. I gingerly remove the faceplate from the chimney and peer inside, usually finding that the bird has gone past the bend in the pipe and is lost somewhere in the darkness on the way to the wood stove. Then the only thing to do is open everything up, including the outside door, in the hope that the starling will eventually find its way back to the open air. More than one bird has met its end in the cold stove because I don't visit the workshop on a daily basis.

On the few occasions when a starling has come down one of the stovepipes in the house, getting rid of them has been more difficult. Of course, the cats and dogs know what is going on, and they arrange themselves nearby in attitudes of breathless anticipation. If the bird can't be grasped firmly as soon as it emerges, there is pandemonium as it flies frantically around the room with the animals in hot pursuit.

DW had an even more exciting experience with a bird in the kitchen chimney. The usual banging and fluttering betrayed the presence of a bird in the pipes. Swearing softly and cursing all starlings, he fetched his leather gloves and prepared to do battle. When he finally got a grip on our unwanted visitor he saw that it was a Wood Duck (*Aix sponsa*), its handsome colouring obscured by soot.

A marsh duck, subfamily *Anatinae*, this is one of our showiest spring birds. In the male of the species the white belly contrasts with the dark brown breast and greenish back. According to Peterson's *Field Guide to the Birds East of the Rockies,* "The bizarre face pattern,

The dirty duck! This Wood Duck came down the kitchen stovepipe, but lived to nest another day.

swept-back crest and rainbow iridescence are unique."[2] The male is patterned in shades of green, purple, and blue.

The Wood Duck can often be seen perching in trees. Like the starling, it is a cavity nester, which no doubt made our kitchen chimney seem attractive, although one would have thought that cold steel would be less comfortable than wood! The Audubon Society's field guide states that the young birds leave the nest soon after hatching, jumping from the nesting cavity to the ground. The roof over the kitchen wing is extremely steep, and it would have been a long way down!

In due course, DW put up a large, wooden nesting box at the creek, and Wood Ducks used this for some years until it was swept away in the spring flood.

---

2. *Field Guide to the Birds East of the Rockies*, 50.

THE HAWK'S CHRISTMAS DINNER

Christmas Eve 2008 brought with it a rare gift in the shape of a Cooper's Hawk, coming to the house for its Christmas dinner. That is to say, it spent several hours patiently waiting for some unwary prey to come into its line of vision, and I had the privilege of watching what was going on barely six feet from my bedroom window.

Cooper's Hawks (*Accipiter cooperi*) have lived on this property for years. I've never succeeded in finding their nest, although I suspect that they usually build one high up in a tree near the creek. Bird books say that two to four eggs may be laid, but I've never seen more than one immature bird in one breeding season.

The winter of 2007–08 provided ample evidence that a hawk was hunting nearby. Once I found a pile of Blue Jay feathers at the bottom of the lane. A few days later, there was a patch of blood and a single feather beneath the bird feeders. When stepping outside en route to the mailbox one morning, I inadvertently flushed an immature Cooper's Hawk out of a basswood tree, where it had been perching in full view of the bird population. I wondered how successful it would be if its prey could see it there.

Early in the morning of Christmas Eve, I looked out to see what the weather was like. Not that it mattered much. Nobody was expected to arrive from far away, and as I had put my car away for the winter, I didn't have to worry about driving conditions. The pond was ice-covered, the fields deeply shrouded in snow. I threw out a supply of bird seed and went to make coffee.

I was surprised when no birds arrived to eat. Usually they clamour outside the windows if I'm late in replenishing supplies. In fact, no matter which room I'm in, they come to those particular windows, somehow knowing where to find me.

Then I saw the hawk, sitting motionless on a branch in a spruce. This is a tree that has grown so close to the house that the tips of its branches come just below my bedroom windowsill. The bird turned its head, gazing back at me. Looking at its red-striped "pajamas," I tried to decide whether this was a Cooper's Hawk or its look-alike, a female Sharp-shinned Hawk. One field mark is the different shape of the tail, but this bird had lost a few feathers, which didn't help. Upon reflection, I decided that the size of the bird, close to that of an American Crow, probably identified it as the Cooper's Hawk. Was it possibly my bird of the previous winter, now grown to maturity?

The hawk stayed on its branch for hours, seldom moving. Every once in a while I returned to my post, to find that nothing had changed. The Blue Jays and squirrels were

A Cooper's Hawk waits for a meal. Sometimes they hunt in full view of other birds yet their patience is rewarded when they swoop down on a blackbird or Blue Jay.

nowhere to be seen. Strangely, a variety of smaller birds — chickadees and nuthatches — flew fearlessly over the hawk's head, and it took no notice. Evidently, it was waiting for something with more meat on it. Feeling sorry for the hungry hawk, I scooped up some raw turkey giblets and threw them into the snow nearby. It looked down for a moment before resuming its original posture. Evidently it preferred warm blood.

By three o'clock, this vigil had been going on for eight hours or more, and I was less patient than the bird. I went away to make a cup of tea. In doing so I missed the kill, for when I came back upstairs the hawk had a Blue Jay on the ground and was busily engaged in plucking it. This was something I'd never seen before! The hawk took a feather in its beak, hopping off the ground in a backwards motion, taking the feather with it before bending to repeat the process. Finally the carcass was bare, and the hawk began its meal.

All this happened in full view of a downstairs window, where Rufus crouched on the sill, tail lashing, as he witnessed what was going on. Unperturbed, the hawk then hopped onto a lower branch, where it rested for some twenty minutes, no doubt "to let the food slip down," as my grandmother used to say. At last, replete, it flew off in the direction of the creek. All in all the operation had gone on from dawn until dusk, and it made my day. My own dinner was woefully late, but what did that matter compared with the gift of participating in a day in the life of a woodland hawk?

Since then, the hawk has returned many times, but I have never again been lucky enough to watch such a performance. Usually a little pile of feathers on the ground is the only evidence that yet another tasty meal has been enjoyed.

THE CUCKOO IN THE THORN BUSH

I was delighted when I heard the call of the Black-billed Cuckoo — *cu cu cu cu!* In part, this was because I looked forward to spotting this uncommon visitor to Poison Ivy Acres, but I was also glad it had come because it eats tent caterpillars. These tents drape many of the small trees, such as wild cherries, and, if left unchecked, the caterpillars soon hatch in large numbers and strip off all the leaves. The cuckoo will also eat the larvae of the Gypsy Moth, which we dread to find here. In all, it is a very welcome arrival.

The Black-billed Cuckoo has a brown back, a plain white breast, and the black, slightly curved beak that gives it its name. It has a narrow red eye ring, which is hard to see unless one is close to the bird. The Black-billed Cuckoo (*Coccyzus erythropthalmus*) is a little larger than the American Robin. In Britain, the cuckoo's behaviour is similar to that of our cowbird, in that it deposits its eggs in other birds' nests, leaving them there for more industrious birds to raise. According to Colin Harrison's *Field Guide to Nests: Eggs and Nestlings,* the Black-billed Cuckoo will do this at times, although members of this species will also build their own nests.

In this case, the bird had gathered twigs and weeds to make a place to raise its own young. I was able to sneak up on it when it was sitting on its nest. It had chosen a small hawthorn tree in a semi-open clearing not far from the house, and the nest was only about four feet off the ground. Later, when the three baby birds had hatched, I was able to peer down on the nest to get a good view of the hatchlings without coming close enough to touch anything, which would have left my scent behind.

Friends from the city came to stay at just the right time to see the fledglings before they left the nest. The visitors had just taken a course on nature photography, so the sighting was just what they needed to practise their newly learned art. When the task was completed to their satisfaction, we continued on our way. That was when our friend's sharp eye noticed something I'd been looking for without success. On my walks along the creek bank, I'd seen a pair of Brown Creepers (*Certhia familiaris*), and I was sure they were nesting somewhere nearby.

These are attractive small brown birds that climb trees spirally from the base up. Their nests are hard to detect because they hide them in a crevice, or behind loose bark on a tree. Jim's sharp eyes noticed the nest, which had been built in a narrow space where the bark was peeling off a tree on the creek bank. It was too inaccessible for us to look inside, but that wasn't important. A mystery had been solved.

The Black-billed Cuckoo is an occasional visitor to Poison Ivy Acres, while the Brown Creeper is found here year-round. Either way, it is thrilling to be able to share their lives for a short period of time.

A RARE DELIGHT

Spring came early to Poison Ivy Acres in 2010. The rhubarb sprang up in March, and the lilacs and the fruit trees blossomed much too soon. Many birds returned early and in greater numbers than usual. I began to think that it would be a good year for birding, but even so, I could hardly believe my eyes when what I thought was a large white turkey dashed across the lane in front of the car, quickly disappearing into the undergrowth. Puzzled, I concluded that it must be an albino bird, but I wanted to have a closer look to make sure.

I spent several fruitless days gazing at groups of our resident Wild Turkeys, without success. Then she — for it was a hen turkey — came into view again, loitering by a small pond, this time accompanied by others whose feathers were the usual brown and golden colours. This slender bird was snowy white, with grey-barred wings and a certain amount of black on the tail.

By mid-May, there were a number of turkey-nesting hollows at the edge of the hayfields, each containing up to a dozen eggs, so I hoped that my pale visitor was among those who laid their eggs there. Could I look forward to seeing more white turkeys in the future? I shall have to wait and see. I have read that this phenomenon skips a generation, although I have yet to verify this. I hope that one of these days we may see white turkeys in the Christmas Bird Count, although they will be hard to spot against a background of snow.

A few weeks later, a pair of Indigo Buntings arrived to delight the eye. In over thirty years, they have been glimpsed on the property only twice, although others have been noted in the district. At first, they perched on a large spruce whose branches touch my bedroom window, that same tree where the hawk had waited patiently for its Christmas dinner. The brown female soon disappeared from view, probably to sit on a nest, but the male, with its glorious turquoise-blue plumage, turned up day after day, hunting for insects. He often found those in the warmth of the south-facing window, while perching momentarily on the protruding window frame, or brushing the glass with beating wings. It was wonderful to be able to study the bunting at such close quarters. Years ago, DW and I attended a spring migration workshop in Texas where we saw hundreds of these lovely birds, along with other species, flying in from Mexico, dropping exhausted into trees along the shore. This was a sight never to be forgotten, and yet, somehow, getting up each morning to see a single Indigo Bunting searching for its breakfast outside my window is even more special.

The days went by, and then something strange and wonderful happened. I was wandering about outside, hoping to locate the buntings' nest, when I looked up to see a most untidy structure which obviously belonged to a much larger bird. Situated about ten feet off the ground, it had been built in the crook of a wooden brace under a permanent wooden awning over the living-room window.

Once indoors, I stood on tiptoe with my head held back, flattening my face against the glass in a desperate attempt to get a closer look. It was impossible to see inside the nest, but I could see a white-splotched tail hanging over the edge. Spots! Cuckoos have spotted tails, but they don't nest in or around houses. On the other hand, their nests are usually about ten feet off the ground, and this one, festooned with loose strands of dried grass, certainly fit the profile.

I went to the other end of the wide window and once again squinted up. As I became accustomed to the gloom, I saw a large, round eye staring down at me, and a sturdy yellow beak, curved down at the end. A Yellow-billed Cuckoo! Later I was able to get a better look at this jay-sized bird when it flew away from the nest. This cuckoo has a white breast and a brown back, with rufous patches on its wings. It was a first for Poison Ivy Acres' life list.

These birds are most beneficial to country dwellers because they feed on caterpillars. They particularly enjoy those destructive tent caterpillars and gypsy moth larvae. I am delighted to welcome these cuckoos to my home!

Charlie and Kate, the first two setters to live at Poison Ivy Acres, were delighted to find a squirrel up a tree. Eventually they had to give up the pursuit as it remained in place, scolding loudly.

APPENDIX A:
BIRDS OF POISON IVY ACRES

Author's Note: The birds on this list are grouped in accordance with the Federation of Ontario Naturalists Field Checklist. Those marked with an asterix were rare sightings on or above the property.

Common Loon (*Gavia immer*)
Great Blue Heron (*Ardea herodias*)
Green Heron (*Butorides striatus*)
Black-crowned Night Heron (*Nycticorax nycticorax*)
American Bittern (*Botaurus lentiginosus*)
Canada Goose (*Branta Canadensis*)
Snow Goose (*Chen caerulescens*) *
Black Brant (*Branta bernicla*) *
Mallard Duck (*Anas platyrhynchos*)
Black Duck (*Anas rubripes*)
Blue-winged Teal (*Anas discors*)
Wood Duck (*Aix sponsa*)
Hooded Merganser (*Lophodytes cucullatus*)
Common Merganser (*Mergus merganser*)
Red-breasted Merganser (*Mergus serrator*)
Turkey Vulture (*Cathartes aura*)
Wild Turkey (*Meleagris gallopavo*)
Sharp-shinned Hawk (*Accipiter striatus*)
Cooper's Hawk (*Accipiter cooperii*)
Northern Goshawk (*Accipiter gentilis*)
Red-tailed Hawk (*Buteo jamaicensis*)
Red-shouldered Hawk (*Buteo lineatus*)
Broad-winged Hawk (*Buteo platypterus*)

Rough-legged Hawk (*Buteo lagopus*)

Bald Eagle (*Haliaeetus leucocephalus*)

Marsh Hawk (Harrier) (*Circus cyaneus*)

Osprey (*Pandion haliaetus*)

Gyrfalcon (*Falco rusticolus*)

Merlin (*Falco columbarius*)

American Kestrel (*Falco sparverius*)

Spruce Grouse (*Canachites canadensis*)

Ruffed Grouse (*Bonasa umbellus*)

Ring-necked Pheasant (*Phasianus colchicus*)*

Gray Partridge (*Perdix perdix*)

Virginia Rail (*Rallus limicola*)

Killdeer (*Charadrius vociferus*)

American Woodcock (*Philohela minor*)

Common Snipe (*Capella gallinago*)

Upland Sandpiper (*Bartramia longicauda*)

Spotted Sandpiper (*Actitis macularia*)

Solitary Sandpiper (*Tringa solitaria*)

Lesser Yellowlegs (*Tringa flavipes*)

Mourning Dove (*Zenaida macroura*)

Black-billed Cuckoo (*Coccyzus erythrothalmus*)

Yellow-billed Cuckoo (*Coccyzus americanus*)

Great Horned Owl (*Bubo virginianus*)

Barred Owl (*Strix varia*)

Long-eared Owl (*Asio otus*)*

Saw-whet Owl (*Aegolius acadicus*)

Hawk Owl (*Surnia ulula*)*

Whip-poor-will (*Caprimulgus vociferus*)

Common Nighthawk (*Chordeiles minor*)

Chimney Swift (*Chaetura pelagica*)

Ruby-throated Hummingbird (*Archilochus colubris*)

Belted Kingfisher (*Megaceryle alcyon*)

Yellow-shafted Flicker (*Colaptes auratus*)

Pileated Woodpecker (*Dryocopus pileatus*)

Yellow-bellied Sapsucker (*Sphyrapicus varius*)

Hairy Woodpecker (*Picoides villosus*)

Downy Woodpecker (*Picoides pubescens*)

Black-backed Three-toed Woodpecker (*Picoides arcticus*)*

Northern Three-toed Woodpecker (*Picoides tridactylus*)*

Eastern Kingbird (*Tyrannus tyrannus*)

Great Crested Flycatcher (*Myiarchus crinitus*)

Eastern Phoebe (*Sayornis phoebe*)

Wood Pewee (*Contopus virens*)

Olive-sided Flycatcher (*Nuttalornis borealis*)

Horned Lark (*Eremophila alpestris*)

Tree Swallow (*Iridoprocne bicolor*)

Barn Swallow (*Hirundo rustica*)

Grey Jay (*Perisoreus canadensis*)

Blue Jay (*Cyanocitta cristata*)

Northern Raven (*Corvus corax*)

Common Crow (*Corvus brachyrhynchos*)

Black-capped Chickadee (*Parus atricapillus*)

Boreal Chickadee (*Parus hudsonicus*)

White-breasted Nuthatch (*Sitta carolinensis*)

Red-breasted Nuthatch (*Sitta canadensis*)

Brown Creeper (*Certhia familiaris*)

House Wren (*Troglodytes aedon*)

Winter Wren (*Troglodytes troglodytes*)*

Gray Catbird (*Dumetella carolinensis*)

Northern Mockingbird (*Mimus polyglottos*)

Brown Thrasher (*Toyostoma rufum*)

American Robin (*Turdus migratorius*)

Wood Thrush (*Hylocichla mustelina*)

Hermit Thrush (*Catharus guttatus*)

Swainson's Thrush (Olive-backed) (*Catharus ustulatus*)

Grey-cheeked Thrush (*Catharus minimus*)

Veery (*Catharus fuscessens*)

Eastern Bluebird (*Sialia sialis*)

Golden-crowned Kinglet (*Regulus satrapa*)
Ruby-crowned Kinglet (*Regulus calendula*)
Bohemian Waxwing (*Bombycilla garrulus*)
Cedar Waxwing (*Bombycilla cedrorum*)
Loggerhead Shrike (*Lanius ludovicianus*)
Northern Shrike (*Lanius excubitor*)
Starling (*Sturnis vulgaris*)
Solitary Vireo (*Vireo solitarius*)
Philadelphia Vireo (*Vireo philadelphicus*)
Red-eyed Vireo (*Vireo olivaceus*)
Yellow-throated Warbler (*Dendroica dominica*)
Black-throated Green Warbler (*Dendroica virens*)
Black-and-white Warbler (*Mniotilter varia*)
Blackpoll Warbler (*Dendroica striata*)
Black-throated Blue Warbler (*Dendroica caerulescens*)
Magnolia Warbler (*Dendroica magnolia*)
Yellow-rumped Warbler (*Dendroica coronata*)
Canada Warbler (*Wilsonia canadensis*)
Cape May Warbler (*Dendroica tigrina*)
Bay-breasted Warbler (*Dendroica castanea*)
Blackburnian Warbler (*Dendroica fusca*)
American Redstart (*Setophaga ruticilla*)
Pine Warbler (*Dendroica pinus*)
Palm Warbler (*Dendroica palmarum*)
Yellow Warbler (*Dendroica petechia*)
Tennessee Warbler (*Vermivora peregrina*)
Orange-crowned Warbler (*Vermivora celata*)
Golden-winged Warbler (*Vermivora chrysoptera*)
Nashville Warbler (*Vermivora ruficapilla*)
Common Yellowthroat (*Geothlypis trichas*)
Northern Waterthrush (*Seiurus noveboracensis*)
Ovenbird (*Seiurus aurocapillus*)
Bobolink (*Dolichonyx oryzivorus*)
Eastern Meadowlark (*Sturnella magna*)

Red-winged Blackbird (*Agelaius phoeniceus*)

Baltimore Oriole (*Icterus galbula*)

Rusty Blackbird (*Euphagus carolinus*)

Common Grackle (*Quiscalus quiscula*)

Brown-headed Cowbird (*Molothrus ater*)

Scarlet Tanager (*Piranga olivacea*)

Northern Cardinal (*Cardinalis cardinalis*)*

Rose-breasted Grosbeak (*Pheucticus ludovicianus*)

Evening Grosbeak (*Hesperiphona vespertina*)

Pine Grosbeak (*Pinicola enucleator*)

Indigo Bunting (*Passerina cyanea*)

Purple Finch (*Carpodacus purpureus*)

Common Redpoll (*Carduelis flammea*)

Hoary Redpoll (*Carduelis hornemann*)

Pine Siskin (*Carduelis pinus*)

American Goldfinch (*Carduelis tristis*)

Red Crossbill (*Loxia curvirostra*)

White-winged Crossbill (*Loxia leucoptera*)

Rufous-sided Towhee (*Pipilo eruthophthalmus*)

Dark-eyed Junco (*Junco hyemalis*)

Vesper Sparrow (*Pooecetes gramineus*)

Tree Sparrow (*Spizza arborea*)

Chipping Sparrow (*Spizza passerina*)

Field Sparrow (*Spizza pusilla*)

White-crowned Sparrow (*Zonotrichia leucophrys*)

White-throated Sparrow (*Zonotrichia albicollis*)

Golden-crowned Sparrow (*Zonotrichia atricapilla*)

Fox Sparrow (*Passerella iliaca*)

Swamp Sparrow (*Melospiza georgiana*)

Song Sparrow (*Melospiza melodia*)

Snow Bunting (*Plectraphenax nivalis*)

APPENDIX B:
TREES OF POISON IVY ACRES

Apple Family (*Malus*)
Sweet Crabapples (*Malus coronaria*)
Flowering Crabapples (*Malus hopa*)
Wild Apples (*Malus sylvestris*)

Ash Family (*Fraxinius*)
White Ash (*Fraxinius americana*)

Birch Family (*Betulaceae*)
Silver (Paper) Birch (*Betula papyrifera*)
Yellow Birch (*Betula alleghaniensis*)

Buckthorn Family (*Rhamnaceae*)
Buckthorn (*Rhamnus cathartica*)

Cashew Family (Sumac) (*Anacardiaceae*)
Poison Sumac (*Toxicodendron vernix*)
Smooth-barked Sumac (*Rhus glabra*)
Staghorn Sumac (*Rhus typhina*)

Cedar Family (*Cupressaceae*)
Northern White Cedar (*Thuja occidentalis*)

Cherry/Plum Family (*Prunus*)
Black Cherry (*Prunus serotina*)
Chokecherry (*Prunus virginiana*)
Gooseberry (*Ribes hirtellum*)
Wild Plum (*Prunus nigra*)

Dogwood Family (*Cornaceae*)
Flowering Dogwood (*Cornus florida*)

Elm Family (*Ulmaceae*)
Cork/Rock Elm (*Ulmas thomasii*)
White Elm (*Ulmas americana*)

Hawthorn Family (*Crataegus*)
Scarlet Hawthorn (*Crataegus coccinea*)

Hazel/Filbert Family (*Corylus*)
Beaked Hazel (*Corylus rostrata*)

Honeysuckle Family (*Caprifoliaceae*)
American Elder (*Sambucus canadensis*)

Hophornbeam Family (*Ostrya*)
Eastern Hophornbeam (Ironwood) (*Ostrya virginiana*)

Hornbeam Family (*Carpinus*)
American Hornbeam (*Carpinus caroliniana*)

Juniper Family (*Juniperus*)
Common Juniper (*Juniperus communis*)

Larch Family (*Larix*)
Tamarack (*Larix larcina*)

Linden Family (*Tiliaceae*)
American Basswood (*Tilia americana*)

Maple Family (*Aceraceae*)
Amur Maple (*Acer ginnala*)
Manitoba Maple (*Acer negundo*)

Sugar Maple (*Acer saccharum*)

Miscellaneous
Highbush Cranberry (*Viburnum trilobum*)
Lilac (*Syringa*)
Common Spindleberry (*Euonymous europaeus*)

Oak Family (*Quercus*)
Bur Oak (*Quercus macrocarpa*)
Northern Red Oak (*Quercus rubra*)
Overcup Oak (*Quercus lyrata*)

Pine Family (*Pinaceae*)
Eastern White Pine (*Pinus strobus*)
Red Pine (*Pinus resinosa*)

Poplars and Aspens (*Populus*)
Balsam Poplar (*Populus balsamifera*)
Black Poplar (Balm of Gilead) (*Populus candicans*)
Quaking Aspen (*Populus tremuloides*)

Rue Family (*Rutaceae*)
Common Prickly Ash (*Zanthoxylum americanum*)

Spruce Family (*Picea*)
White Spruce (*Picea glauca*)

True Firs (*Abies*)
Balsam Fir (*Abies balsamea*)

Willow Family (*Salicaceae*)
Pussy Willow (*Salix discolor*)
Swamp Willow (*Salix canadensis*)

APPENDIX C:
WILDFLOWERS OF POISON IVY ACRES

Arum Family (*Araceae*)
Jack-in-the-pulpit (*Arisaema triphyllum*)

Bedstraw Family (*Rubiaceae*)
Bluets (*Houstonia caerlea*)

Bluebell Family (*Campanulaceae*)
Creeping Bellflower (*Campanula rapunculoides*) Purple
Harebell (*Campanula rotundiflolia*) Mauve

Buckwheat Family (*Polygonaceae*)
Curled Dock (*Rumex crispus*)
Lady's Thumb (*Polygonum persicaris*)
Sheep Sorrel (*Rumex acetosella*)

Buttercup/Crowfoot Family (*Ranunculaceae*)
Columbine (*Aquilegia canadensis*) Red and yellow
Common Buttercup (*Ranunculus acris*) Yellow
Early Meadow Rue (*Thalictrum dioicum*) White
Marsh Marigold (*Caltha palustris*) Yellow
Round-lobed Hepatica (*Hepatica americana*) Mauve, pink, white
Rue-anemone (*Anemonella thalictroides*) White
Virgin's Bower (*Clematis virginiana*) (also known as Traveller's Joy; Wild Clematis;
    Old Man's Beard)
White Baneberry (*Actaea pachypoda*) (Doll's Eyes)
Wood Anemone (*Anemone quinquefolia*)

Cattail Family (*Typhaceae*)
Common Cattail (*Typha latifolia*)

Composite/Daisy Family (*Compositae*)
Beggar-ticks (*Bidens frondosa*)
Boneset (*Eupatorium perfolia tum*)
Calico Aster (*Aster lateriflorus*)
Canada Hawkweed (*Hieracium canadensis*) Yellow
Canada Thistle (*Cirsium arvense*)
Chicory (*Cichorium intybus*) Pale blue
Coltsfoot (*Tussilago farfara*)
Common Fleabane (*Erigeron philadelphicus*) Pinkish
Common Ragweed (*Artemissifolia*) Yellow
Common Tansy (*Tanacetum vulgare*)
Dandelion (*Taraxacumn officinale*)
Golden Ragwort (*Senecio aureus*)
Goldenrod (*Solidago*) several varieties
Heart-leaved Aster (*Aster corifolius*)
New England Aster (*Aster Novae-angliae*)
Orange Hawkweed (*Heiracium aurantiacum*) Devil's Paintbrush
Ox-eye Daisy (*Chrysanthemum leucanthemum*)
Pearly Everlasting (*Anaphalis magaritacea*) White
Prickly Lettuce (*Lactuca scariola*)
Ragwort (*Senecio aureus*)
Scotch Thistle (*Onopordum acanthium*)
Smaller Pussy-toes (*Antennia neodioica*) White
Spotted Joe-Pye Weed (*Eupatorium maculatam*) Red
Stiff Aster (*Aster linearifolius*)
Yarrow (*Achillea millefolium*) White, pink, green
Yellow Goat's Beard (*Tragopogon dubius*)

Dogbane Family (*Apocynaceae*)
Spreading Dogbane (*Apocynum androsaemilifolium*) Pink and white

Dogwood Family (*Cornaceae*)
Bunchberry (*Cornus canadensis*)

Evening Primrose Family (*Onagraceae*)
Common Evening Primrose (*Oenothera biennis*)
Fireweed (*Epilobium angustifolium*)

Forget-me-not Family (*Boraginaceae*)
Corn Gromwell (*Lithospermium arvense*)
Smaller Forget-me-not (*Myosotis laxa*)
Viper's Bugloss (*Echium vulgare*)
Virginia Bluebells (*Mertensia virginica)*

Gentian Family (*Gentianaceae*)
Closed (Bottle) Gentian (*Gentian andresii*)
Fringed Gentian (*Gentiana crinita*)

Geranium Family (*Geraniaceae*)
Herb Robert (*Geranium robertianum*)

Goosefoot Family (*Chenopodiaceae*)
Pigweed (*Chenopodium album*) (also known as Lamb's Quarters) Green
Strawberry-blite (*Chenopodium capitatum*) Red

Indian Pipe Family (*Monotropaceae*)
Indian Pipe (*Monotropa uniflora*)

Iris Family (*Iridaceae*)
Blue Flag (*Iris versicolor*)
Yellow Flag (*Iris pseudaconis*)

Lily Family (*Liliaceae*)
Day Lily (*Hemerocallus fulva*) Orange
Large-flowered Bellwort (*Uvularia grandiflora*) Yellow

Solomon's Seal (*Polygonatum biflorum*) Yellow
Purple Trillium (*Trillium erectum*) (also known as Wakerobin)
Trout Lily (*Erythronium americanum*) Yellow
White Trillium (*Trillium grandiflorum*)
Wild Leek (*Allium tricoccum*)
Wild Lily of the Valley (*Maianthemum canadence*) (also known as Canada Mayflower)

Lobelia Subfamily (*Lobelioideae*) (See Bluebell Family)
Cardinal Flower (*Lobelia cardinalis*)
Indian Tobacco (*Lobelia inflata*)
Longleaf Lobelia (*Lobelia eleongata*)

Loosestrife Family (*Lythraceae*)
Purple Loosestrife (*Lythrum salicaria*)

Mallow Family (*Malvaceae*)
Cheeses (*Malva neglecta*)
Musk Mallow (*Malva moschala*)

Milkweed Family (*Asclepiadaceae*)
Common Milkweed (*Asclepias syriaca*)
Four-leaved Milkweed (*Asclepias quadrifolia*)
Purple Milkweed (*Asclepias purpurascens*)

Mint Family (*Labiatae*)
All Heal (*Prunella vulgaris*)
American Pennyroyal (*Hedcoma pulegionides*)
Bugle (*Ajuga reptans*)
Catnip (*Nepeta cataria*)
Downy Wood-mint (*Blephilia ciliata*)
Ground Ivy (*Glechoma hederacea*)
Red Deadnettle (*Lamium tenuifolia*)
Rough Hedgenettle (*Stachys tenuifolia*)
Wild Mint (*Mentha arvensis*)

Morning Glory Family (*Convolvulaceae*)
Field Bindweed (*Convolvulus arvensis*) White

Mustard Family (*Cruciferae*)
Dame's Rocket (*Hesperis matronalis*) Deep pink
Field Mustard (*Brassica rapa*)
Field Pennycress (*Thlaspi arvense*)
Shepherd's Purse (*Capsella bursa-pastoris*)

Nettle Family (*Urticaceae*)
Stinging Nettle (*Urtica dioica*)

Nightshade Family (*Solanaceae*)
Clammy Ground Cherry (*Physalis heterophyllo*)
Deadly Nightshade (*Solanum dulcamara*)

Orchid Family (*Orchidaceae*)
Helleborine (*Epipactis helleborine*)
Yellow Lady's Slipper (*Cypripedium calceolus*)

Parsley/Carrot Family (*Umbelliferae*)
Cow Parsnip (*Heracleum maximum*)
Queen Anne's Lace (*Daucus carota*) (also known as Wild Carrot)
Sweet Cicely (*Osmorhiza claytoni*)
Water Hemlock (*Cicuta maculata*)
Wild Parsnip (*Pastinaca sativa*)

Pea Family (*Leguminosae*)
Alfalfa (*Medicago sativa*)
Black Medick (*Medicago lupulina*)
Hop Clover (*Trifolium agraium*)
Purple Vetch (*Vicia americana*)
Red Clover (*Trifolium pratense*)
White Sweet Clover (*Meliotus alba*)

Yellow Sweet Clover (*Meliotis officinalis*)

Phlox Family (*Polemoniacceae*)
Blue Phlox (*Phlox divaricata*)

Pink Family (*Caryophyllaceae*)
Bladder Campion (*Silene cucubalas*)
Bouncing Bet/Soapwort (*Saponaria officinalis*) Pink
Field Chickweed (*Cerastium arvensi*)

Plantain Family (*Plantaginaceae*)
English Plantain (*Plantago lanceolata*)

Poppy Family (*Papaveraceae*)
Bloodroot (*Sanguinaria canadensis*)
Celandine (*Chelidonium majus*)
Dutchman's Breeches (*Dicetra cucullaris*)

Primrose Family (*Primulaceae*)
Starflower (*Trientalis borealis*)

Purslane Family (*Portulacaceae*)
Purslane (*Portulaca oleracea*)
Spring Beauty (*Claytonia viginica*) Pink striped

Rose Family (*Rosaceae*)
Barren Strawberry (*Waldsteinia fragarioides*)
Brambles (*Rubus*)
Common Cinquefoil (*Potentilla simplex*)
Common Strawberry (*Fragaria virginiana*)
Pasture Rose (*Rosa carolina*)
Purple-flowering Raspberry (*Rubus odoraturs*)
Silver Cinquefoil (*Potentilla argentea*)
Steeplebush (*Spiraea tomentosa*)

Snapdragon Family (*Scrophulariaceae*)
Beardtongue (*Penstemon hirsutus*)
Bird's-eye Speedwell (*Veronica chamaedrys*)
Common Mullein (*Verbascum thapsus*)
Monkeyflower (*Mimulus ringens*)
Turtlehead (*Chelona glabra*) White.
Wood-Betony (*Pedicularis canadensis*)
Yellow Toadflax (*Linaria vulgaris*) **(also known as Butter and Eggs)**

St. John's Wort Family (*Guttiferae*)
Common St. John's Wort (*Hypericum perforatum*)

Teasel Family (*Dipsacaceae*)
Field Scabious (*Knautia arvensis*)
Teasel (*Dipsacus sylvestris*)

Tomato Family (Nightshade Family) **(*Solanaceae*)**
Jimsonweed (*Datura stramonium*)

Touch-me-not Family (*Balsaminaceae*)
Jewelweed (*Impatiens capensis*) (also known as Spotted Touch-me-not)

Vervain Family (*Verbenaceae*)
Narrow-leaved Vervain (*Verbena simplex*)

Violet Family (*Violaceae*)
Canada Violet (*Viola canadensis*)
Common Blue Violet (*Viola papilionacea*)
Dog Violet (*Viola consperga*)
Northern White Violet (*Viola pallens*)
Round-leaved Yellow Violet (*Viola rotunifolia*)

Waterlily Family (*Nymphaeceae*)
Fragrant Waterlily (*Nymphaea odorata*)

Wintergreen Family (*Pyrolaceae*)
Indian Pipe (*Monotropa uniflora*)

The harvest is in! DW proudly displays his potato crop.

BIBLIOGRAPHY

There are several shelves of nature reference books at Poison Ivy Acres, but the following are the most popular.

Dagg, Anne Innis. *Mammals of Ontario*. Waterloo, ON: Otter Press, 1974.

Fenton, M. Brock. *Just Bats*. Toronto: University of Toronto Press, 1983.

Froom, Barbara. *The Snakes of Canada*. Toronto: McClelland & Stewart Ltd., 1972.

Glick, Phyllis. *The Mushroom Trail Guide*. New York: Holt, Rinehart & Winston, 1979.

Godfrey, W. Earl. *The Birds of Canada*. Ottawa: National Museums of Canada, 1986. Revised edition.

Harrison, Colin. *A Field Guide to Nests, Eggs and Nestlings*. Toronto: Collins, 1978.

Headstrom, Richard. *Whose Track Is It?* New York: Ives Washburn Inc., 1971.

Hines, Bob. *Ducks at a Distance: A Waterfowl Identification Guide*. Ottawa: Canadian Wildlife Service, 1969.

Lawrence, R.D. *The Place in the Forest*. Toronto: Natural Heritage Books, 1998.

Mackenzie, Katherine. *Wild Flowers of Eastern Canada*. Montreal: Tundra Books, 1973.

Pimlott, D.H., J.A. Shannon, and G.B. Kolenosky. *The Ecology of the Timber Wolf in Algonquin Provincial Park*. Research Branch, Department of Lands & Forests, 1969.

Sheldon, Ian. *Animal Tracks of Ontario*. Vancouver: Lone Pine Publishing, 1997.

Theberge, John B. *Wolves & Wilderness*. Toronto: M. Dent & Sons, 1975.

Van Camp, J.L. *Fifty Trees of Canada East of the Rockies*. Toronto: The Book Society of Canada, 1952.

Wolves and Coyotes of Ontario. Ontario Department of Lands and Forests, nd.

Wooding, Frederick H. *Wild Mammals of Canada*. Toronto: McGraw-Hill Ryerson, 1982.

Field Guides

(1) The Peterson Field Guides, Boston: Houghton Mifflin Company.

Borror, Donald J, and Richard E. White. *A Field Guide to the Insects: America North of Mexico*, 1970.

Conant, Roger. *A Field Guide to Reptiles and Amphibians*, 1958.

Klots, Alexander B. *A Field Guide to the Butterflies of North America East of the Great Plains.* 1951.

Peterson, Lee Allen. *A Field Guide to Edible Wild Plants of Eastern and Central North America.* 1977.

Peterson, Roger Tory. *A Field Guide to the Birds*, 1980.

Peterson, Roger Tory, and Margaret McKenny. *A Field Guide to the Wildflowers of North Eastern and North Central North America.* 1968.

(2) The Audubon Society Field Guides. New York: Chanticleer Press, Albert A. Knopf.

Bull, John, and John J. Farrand. *The Audubon Society Field Guide to North American Birds, Eastern Region.* 1977.

Chesterman, Charles W. *The Audubon Society Field Guide to North American Rocks and Minerals.* 1978.

Lincoff, Gary H. *The Audubon Society Field Guide to North American Mushrooms.* 1981.

Little, Elbert L. *The Audubon Society Field Guide to North American Trees.* 1980.

Milne, Lorus and Margery. *The Audubon Society Field Guide to North American Insects and Spiders.* 1980.

Niering, William A., and Nancy C. Olmstead. *The Audubon Society Field Guide to North American Wildflowers, Eastern Region.* 1979.

Pyle, Robert Michael. *The Audubon Society Field Guide to North American Butterflies.* 1981.

Whitaker, John O. Jr. *The Audubon Society Field Guide to North American Mammals.* 1980.

(3) Golden Field Guides. New York: Golden Press.

Brockman, C. Frank. *Trees of North America.* 1968.

Robbins, Chandler S., Bertel Bruun, and Herbert S. Zim. *Birds of North America.* 1966.

INDEX

ABOUT THE AUTHOR

CAROL BENNETT McCUAIG of Renfrew County is a former weekly newspaper editor and a graduate of the University of Waterloo. She writes both fiction and non-fiction. In 1997, she received an Achievement Award from the Ontario Heritage Foundation for her body of work in recording regional history. Her novels are published in Britain under the pseudonym Catriona McCuaig. *Encountering the Wild* is her fiftieth book.

ABOUT THE PHOTOGRAPHER

DW McCUAIG (1923–89) owned a chain of weekly newspapers in Ontario until 1978, and established Juniper Books, publishing regional history. He enjoyed photographing wildlife in Kenya and the Canadian Arctic.

THE LURE OF FARAWAY PLACES
Reflections on Wilderness and Solitude
by Herb Pohl
918-1897045244
$27.95

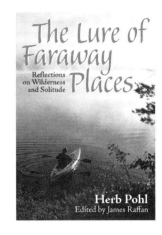

Pohl's words and images provide a unique portrait of Canada by one who was happiest when travelling our northern waterways alone. Austrian-born Herb Pohl died at the mouth of the Michipcoten River on July 17, 2006. He is remembered as "Canada's most remarkable solo traveller." While mourning their loss, Herb Pohl's friends found, to their surprise and delight, a manuscript of wilderness writings on his desk in his lakeside apartment in Burlington, Ontario. He had hoped one day to publish his work as a book. With help and commentary from best-selling canoe author and editor James Raffan, Herb's book has finally taken shape as *The Lure of Faraway Places*. "There's nothing like it in canoeing literature," says Raffan. "It's part journal, part memoir, part wilderness philosophy and part tips and tricks of the most pragmatic kind written about parts of the country most of us will never see, by the most committed and ambitious solo canoeist in Canadian history."

NATURE FIRST
Outdoor Life the Friluftsliv Way
edited by Bob Henderson and Nils Vikander
978-155002743
$29.99

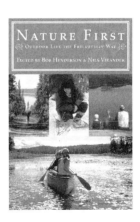

Nature First combines the Scandinavian approach to creating a relationship with nature (known as *friluftsliv*) with efforts by Canadian and international educators to adapt this wisdom and apply it to everyday life experiences in the open air. The word *friluftsliv* literally refers to "free-air life" or outdoor life. A word saturated with values, the concept can permeate deeply and playfully into one's cultural being and personal psyche, thus influencing the way one perceives and interacts with nature on a daily basis. *Nature First* is the first English-language anthology to bring together the perspectives and experiences of North American, Norwegian, Swedish, and other international outdoor writers, all *friluftsliv* thinkers and doers. Here, the thirty contributors' use of history, sociology, psychology, philosophy, and outdoor education writings blend to provide an understanding of how *friluftsliv* applies to everyday life.

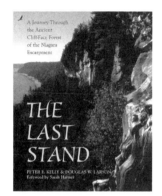

THE LAST STAND
A Journey Through the Ancient Cliff-Face Forest of the Niagara Escarpment
by Peter E. Kelly and Douglas W. Larson
978-897045190
$39.95

The most ancient and least disturbed forest ecosystem in eastern North America clings to the vertical cliffs of the Niagara Escarpment. Prior to 1988, it had escaped detection even though the entire forest was in plain view and was being visited by thousands upon thousands of people every year. The reason no one had discovered the forest was that the trees were relatively small and lived on the vertical cliffs of the Niagara Escarpment. *The Last Stand* reveals the complete account of the discovery of this ancient forest, of the miraculous properties of the trees forming this forest (eastern white cedar), and of what is was like for researchers to live, work, and study within this forest. The unique story is told with text, with stunning colour photographs, and through vivid first-hand accounts. This book will stand the test of time as a testament to science, imagination, and discovery.